What readers are saying about
tmux 2: Productive Mouse-Free Development

A must-have book for anyone that uses the command line daily. This is a book I have been recommending since it was first published, and I will definitely recommend it again!

➤ **Jeff Holland**
   Senior software engineer, Ackmann & Dickenson

The tricks mentioned in this book completely changed my workflow. I recommend this book to anyone who is looking to improve their workflow on the command line.

➤ **Jacob Chae**
   Software engineer, Assurant

The author always has something amazing in store for you: custom commands to fire up your development environment, customizing it, pair programming, and many use cases. This book makes you step up your game in becoming a more efficient developer.

➤ **Peter Perlepes**
   Software engineer, adaplo

I had zero tmux experience before picking up the book, and I could use tmux in my day-to-day routine after reading the book.

➤ **Nick McGinness**
   Software engineer, Direct Supply

tmux 2

Productive Mouse-Free Development

Brian P. Hogan

The Pragmatic Bookshelf

Raleigh, North Carolina

Many of the designations used by manufacturers and sellers to distinguish their products are claimed as trademarks. Where those designations appear in this book, and The Pragmatic Programmers, LLC was aware of a trademark claim, the designations have been printed in initial capital letters or in all capitals. The Pragmatic Starter Kit, The Pragmatic Programmer, Pragmatic Programming, Pragmatic Bookshelf, PragProg and the linking *g* device are trademarks of The Pragmatic Programmers, LLC.

Every precaution was taken in the preparation of this book. However, the publisher assumes no responsibility for errors or omissions, or for damages that may result from the use of information (including program listings) contained herein.

Our Pragmatic books, screencasts, and audio books can help you and your team create better software and have more fun. Visit us at *https://pragprog.com.*

The team that produced this book includes:

Development Editor: Susannah Davidson Pfalzer
Copy Editor: Nicole Abramowitz
Layout: Gilson Graphics
Producer: Janet Furlow

For sales, volume licensing, and support, please contact *support@pragprog.com.*

For international rights, please contact *rights@pragprog.com.*

ISBN-13: 978-1-68050-221-3
Book version: P2.0—September 2018

Contents

Acknowledgments vii
Preface ix

1. **Learning the Basics** 1
   Installing tmux   1
   Starting tmux   3
   The Command Prefix   4
   Detaching and Attaching Sessions   5
   Working with Windows   8
   Working with Panes   9
   Working with Command Mode   11
   What's Next?   12
   For Future Reference   12

2. **Configuring tmux** 15
   Introducing the .tmux.conf File   15
   Customizing Keys, Commands, and User Input   18
   Visual Styling   22
   Customizing the Status Line's Content   28
   What's Next?   31
   For Future Reference   31

3. **Scripting Customized tmux Environments** 35
   Creating a Custom Setup with tmux Commands   35
   Using tmux Configuration for Setup   40
   Managing Configuration with tmuxinator   41
   What's Next?   44
   For Future Reference   45

4. **Working With Text and Buffers** 47
   Scrolling Through Output with Copy Mode   47

Copying and Pasting Text   48

Working with the Clipboard on Linux   51

Using macOS Clipboard Commands   52

What's Next?   53

For Future Reference   53

5.   **Pair Programming with tmux**   55

Pairing with a Shared Account   56

Using a Shared Account and Grouped Sessions   57

Quickly Pairing with tmate   58

Pairing with Separate Accounts and Sockets   60

What's Next?   62

For Future Reference   62

6.   **Workflows**   63

Working Effectively with Panes and Windows   63

Managing Sessions   66

tmux and Your Operating System   68

Extending tmux with Plugins   73

What's Next?   74

For Future Reference   74

A1.   **Our Configuration**   77

Acknowledgments

Thank you for reading this book. It's my sincere hope that this book will help you get better at what you do by making you faster and more productive.

Thank you, Chris Johnson, for initially showing me what tmux was all about, and for pointing me in the right direction with my initial questions. It completely changed how I work, and it's what motivated me to share this amazing tool with everyone.

Thank you, Dave Thomas, for convincing me to publish the first edition of this book. I'm very proud of the first edition and how many people it helped. And thank you, Andy Hunt and Janet Furlow, for all the work you do to deliver the best technical books out there.

Thank you, Susannah Pfalzer, for working with me again. You challenged me once again to grow as an author, and this book and I are better for it.

Thank you, Alessandro Bahgat, Jacob Chae, Jeff Holland, Michael Hunter, Sean Lindsay, Lokesh Kumar Makani, Nick McGinness, Stephen Orr, Peter Perlepes, Charley Stran, and Colin Yates, for reviewing this book. The second edition is more clear and has better explanations because of the time you took to read through this book and try out every example. Anything that's still broken is my fault.

Thank you to my business associates, Mitch Bullard, Kevin Gisi, Alex Henry, Jeff Holland, Nick LaMuro, Austen Ott, Erich Tesky, Myles Steinhauser, Josh Swan, Chris Warren, and Mike Weber, for your continued support.

Thank you, Ana and Lisa, for your love and inspiration.

Finally, thank you, Carissa, for your love and support. Thank you for all you do for our family.

Preface

Your mouse is slowing you down.

When it was first introduced, the mouse created a new way for people to interact with computers. We can click, double-click, and even triple-click to open documents, switch windows, and select text. And thanks to trackpads, we can even swipe and use gestures to interact with our applications. The mouse, along with graphical interfaces, made computers just a little easier to use for the average person. But there's a downside to the mouse, especially for programmers.

As we build software, we work with multiple programs throughout the course of our day. A web developer, for example, might have a database console, a web server, and a text editor running at the same time. Switching between these with the mouse can slow you down. It may not seem like much, but moving your hand off of the keyboard's home row, placing it on the mouse, locating the pointer, and performing the task can eat up time and break your focus. And it can also induce strain on your wrist, arm, or shoulder. That repetitive movement of reaching for your mouse can cause some serious discomfort if you're not careful about how you hold that mouse.

Using tmux, you can create an environment like this, right in your terminal, managed entirely without a mouse:

Using tmux's windows, you can easily manage a text editor, a database console, and a local web server within a single environment. And you can split tmux windows into sections, so multiple apps can run side by side. This means you can run a text-based browser, an IRC client, or your automated tests in the same window as your main editor.

Best of all, you can quickly move between these windows and panes using only the keyboard. Over time, the keystrokes you use to manage your environment will become second nature to you, which will greatly increase both your concentration and your productivity.

In this book, you'll learn how to configure, use, and customize tmux. You'll learn how to manage multiple programs simultaneously, write scripts to create custom environments, and use tmux to work remotely with others. With tmux, you can create a work environment that keeps almost everything you need at your fingertips.

What Is tmux?

tmux is a *terminal multiplexer*. It lets you use a single environment to launch multiple terminals, or windows, each running its own process or program. For example, you can launch tmux and load up the Vim text editor. You can then create a new window, load up a database console, and switch back and forth between these programs all within a single session.

If you use a modern operating system and a terminal that has tabs, this doesn't sound like anything new. But running multiple programs simultaneously is only one of tmux's features. You can divide your terminal windows into horizontal or vertical panes, which means you can run two or more programs on the same screen side by side. And you can do it all without using the mouse.

You can also *detach* from a session, meaning you can leave your environment running in the background. If you've used GNU-Screen before, you're familiar with this feature. In many ways, tmux is like GNU-Screen with a lot of extra features and a much simpler configuration system. And since tmux uses a client-server model, you can control windows and panes from a central location, or even jump between multiple sessions from a single terminal window. This client-server model also lets you create scripts and interact with tmux from other windows or applications.

Over the course of this book, you'll explore all of these features and more.

Who Should Read This Book

Whether you're a system administrator or a software developer who spends a good part of your time using the terminal and command-line tools, this book aims to help you work faster.

If you're a software developer, you'll see how to use tmux to build a development environment that can make working with multiple terminal sessions a breeze. And if you're already comfortable using Vim or Emacs, you'll see how tmux can accelerate your workflow even more.

If you're a system administrator or a developer who spends some time working with remote servers, you'll be interested in how you can leverage tmux to create a persistent dashboard for managing or monitoring servers.

What's in This Book

This book will help you incorporate tmux into your work by taking you through its basic features and showing you how you can apply them to everyday situations.

In Chapter 1, *Learning the Basics*, on page 1, you'll use tmux's basic features. You'll create sessions, panes, and windows and learn how to perform basic navigation.

In Chapter 2, *Configuring tmux*, on page 15, you'll redefine many of the default keybindings and customize how tmux looks.

In Chapter 3, *Scripting Customized tmux Environments*, on page 35, you'll script your own development environment using the command-line interface, configuration files, and the tmuxinator program.

After that, you'll work with text in Chapter 4, *Working With Text and Buffers*, on page 47. You'll use the keyboard to move backwards through the buffer, select and copy text, and work with multiple paste buffers. You'll also integrate tmux with your system clipboard.

Next, in Chapter 5, *Pair Programming with tmux*, on page 55, you'll set up tmux so that you and a coworker can work together on the same codebase from different computers using tmux.

Finally, Chapter 6, *Workflows*, on page 63 covers more advanced ways to manage windows, panes, and sessions, and shows you how to be even more productive with tmux.

Changes in the Second Edition

This new edition has some notable changes from the first edition. tmux 2.1, 2.2, and 2.6 introduced several backwards-incompatible changes that this edition addresses; this edition also introduces some new options. And tmux is now more popular than it was, so there are more tools and tricks you can use to improve your workflow. Here's what's new:

- All examples in this edition require at least tmux 2.6. Previous versions use different configuration syntax for many options.

- This book now covers installation on Windows 10, where tmux is supported under Microsoft's Windows Subsystem for Linux, provided you are using the Creators Edition released in April of 2017 or later, and are using Ubuntu.

- Chapter 2, *Configuring tmux*, on page 15 includes more options for identifying the active pane, uses more updated methods for controlling tmux's visual styles, and removes some outdated configuration options that no longer work.

- Chapter 3, *Scripting Customized tmux Environments*, on page 35 contains updated instructions for Tmuxinator and its new configuration format, as well as information on how to export tmux scripts from Tmuxinator.

- Chapter 4, *Working With Text and Buffers*, on page 47 has an updated method for getting text to and from system clipboards on Linux and Mac. It covers the keybindings for copy mode introduced in tmux 2.4 and higher.

- Chapter 5, *Pair Programming with tmux*, on page 55 now includes instructions on generating an SSH key, and discusses how to use tmate as a quick alternative.

- Chapter 6, *Workflows*, on page 63 contains several new sections:

  - *Opening a Pane in the Current Directory*, on page 65

  - *Keeping Specific Configuration Separate*, on page 69

  - *Integrating Seamlessly with Vim*, on page 72

  - *Extending tmux with Plugins*, on page 73

What You Need

In order to use tmux, you'll need a computer that runs macOS, Windows 10 with Bash support, or a flavor of Unix or Linux. Unfortunately, tmux doesn't run under the regular Windows Command Prompt or Powershell, but it will run great on a virtual machine, VPS, cloud, or shared hosting environment running Linux or FreeBSD.

You should also have a good grasp of using command-line tools on a macOS, Linux, or Unix-like system. We'll use the Bash shell in this book, and being comfortable with creating directories and text files, as well as some basic scripting, will help you move more quickly through the examples.

While not required, experience with text editors such as Vim or Emacs might be helpful. tmux works much the same way, and it has some predefined keyboard shortcuts that you may find familiar if you use one of these text editors.

Conventions

tmux is a tool that's driven by the keyboard. You'll encounter many keyboard shortcuts throughout the book. Since tmux supports both lowercase and uppercase keyboard shortcuts, it may sometimes be unclear which key the book is referencing.

To keep it simple, these are the conventions I've used.

- `Ctrl`-`b` means "press the `Ctrl` and `b` keys simultaneously."

- `Ctrl`-`R` means you'll press the `Ctrl` and `r` keys simultaneously, but you'll need to use the `Shift` key to produce the capital "R." I won't explicitly show the `Shift` key in any of these keystrokes.

- `Ctrl`-`b` `d` means "press the `Ctrl` and `b` keys simultaneously, then release, and then press `d`." In Chapter 1, *Learning the Basics*, on page 1, you'll learn about the *command prefix*, which will use this notation, but shortened to `Prefix` `d`.

- I'll show some terminal commands throughout the book, like

  ```
  $ tmux new-session
  ```

  The dollar sign represents the prompt from the Bash shell session. You won't need to type it when you type the command. It just denotes that this is a command you should type.

- Finally, as you'll see in Chapter 2, *Configuring tmux*, on page 15, you can configure tmux with a configuration file in your home directory called .tmux.conf. Filenames starting with a period don't show up in directory listings on most systems or text editors by default. Code listings in this book have a header that points to the file in the book's source code download, like this:

```
config/tmux.conf
# Setting the prefix from C-b to C-a
set -g prefix C-a
```

To make it easy for you to find the file in the source code download, I've named the example file tmux.conf, without the leading period. The headers above the code listing reference that file.

Online Resources

The book's website[1] has links to submit errata for the book as well as the source code for the configuration files and scripts we use in this book. You can click the box above the code excerpts to download that source code directly.

Working with tmux has made me much more productive, and I'm excited to share my experiences with you. Let's get started by installing tmux and working with its basic features.

---

1. http://pragprog.com/titles/bhtmux2

## CHAPTER 1

Learning the Basics

tmux can be an incredible productivity booster once you get the hang of it. In this chapter, you'll get acquainted with tmux's basic features as you manage applications within sessions, windows, and panes. These simple concepts make up the foundation of what makes tmux an amazing environment for developers and system administrators alike.

But before you can learn how to use these basic features, you need to get tmux installed.

Installing tmux

You can install tmux in one of two ways: using a package manager for your operating system, or building tmux from source.

Whichever method you choose, you'll want to ensure you install tmux version 2.2 or higher. Earlier versions of tmux don't support some of the features we're going to cover in this book, or have configuration that's incompatible.

Installing on a Mac

The easiest way to install tmux on the Mac is with Homebrew.[1]

First, install Xcode through the Mac App Store. Once Xcode is installed, open a new terminal and run the command

```
$ xcode-select --install
```

to install the command-line tools that Homebrew needs.

Next, install Homebrew by following the instructions on the Homebrew website.

---

1. http://brew.sh

Finally, install tmux with the following terminal command:

```
$ brew install tmux
```

To ensure that tmux is installed properly, and to check that you have the correct version, execute this command from your terminal:

```
$ tmux -V
tmux 2.7
```

Installing on Windows 10

Windows 10 has a feature called the Windows Subsystem for Linux. When enabled, you're able to run a Linux distribution on Windows. This gives you access to a Bash shell which can run tmux. To use it, first ensure you're running Windows 10 build 1607 or higher.

Next, enable WSL by opening the Control Panel and selecting Programs. Then click Turn Windows Features On Or Off. Locate and enable the option for "Windows Subsystem For Linux." Then reboot your computer.

When the computer reboots, open the Windows Store and search for Ubuntu. Download Ubuntu to your machine and launch it. A console window will appear, indicating that Ubuntu is installing. Once it finishes, you'll be prompted to create a user. You can use the same username as your Windows user or choose something completely different. This use is separate from your regular Windows account.

Once Bash is installed, move on to the next section, as you'll install tmux from source as if you were using Ubuntu.

Installing on Linux

On Linux, your best bet is to install tmux by downloading the source code and compiling it yourself. Package managers don't always have the most recent version of tmux available. The process of installing tmux is the same on all platforms. You'll need the GCC compiler, and libevent and ncurses, which tmux depends on.

For Ubuntu, you can install all of these with the apt package manager:

```
$ sudo apt-get install build-essential libevent-dev libncurses-dev
```

Once you have the compilers and prerequisites installed, grab the tmux source code and download it.[2] Untar the downloaded version and install it like this:

```
$ tar -zxvf tmux-2.6.tar.gz
$ cd tmux-2.6
$ ./configure
$ make
$ sudo make install
```

You can test out the installation by executing this from the terminal, which returns the currently installed version of tmux:

```
$ tmux -V
tmux 2.6
```

Now that you have tmux properly installed, let's explore the core features of tmux, starting with a basic session.

Starting tmux

Starting tmux is as easy as typing

```
$ tmux
```

from a terminal window. You'll see something that looks like the following image appear on your screen.

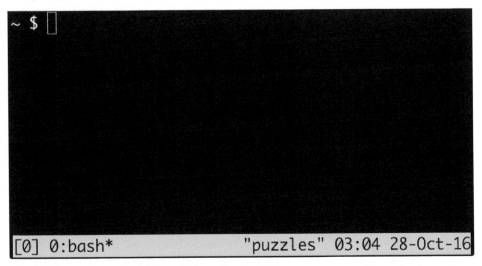

This is a tmux "session," and it works just like your normal terminal session. You can issue any terminal command you'd like, and everything will work as expected.

---

2.   https://tmux.github.io/

To close the tmux session, simply type

```
$ exit
```

in the session itself. This will close tmux and then return you to the standard terminal.

But, unless you're only using tmux for a very brief period, this isn't the best way to work with sessions in tmux. You can instead create "named sessions" that you can then identify and work with later.

Creating Named Sessions

You can have multiple sessions on a single computer, and you'll want to be able to keep them organized. For example, you might have one session for each application you're developing, or a session for work and a session for your cool side project. You can keep these sessions organized by giving each session you create its own unique name. Try it out right now. Create a named session called "basic" with the following command:

```
$ tmux new-session -s basic
```

You can shorten this command to

```
$ tmux new -s basic
```

When you enter this command, you'll be brought into a brand-new tmux session, but you won't really notice anything special or different than if you started things up normally. If you typed exit, you'd just be right back at the terminal. Named sessions come in handy when you want to leave tmux running in the background, which we'll discuss shortly. But before you continue, type

```
$ exit
```

to exit tmux.

Before we look at how to work with tmux sessions and run programs in the background, let's talk about how we send commands to tmux.

The Command Prefix

Since our command-line programs run inside tmux, we need a way to tell tmux that the command we're typing is for tmux and not for the underlying application. The `Ctrl-b` combination does just that. This combination is called the *command prefix*.

You prefix each tmux command with this key combination. To get a feel for how this works, open tmux again:

```
$ tmux
```

Then, inside of tmux, press `Ctrl-b`, then press `t`. A large clock will appear on the screen.

It's important to note that you don't hold all these keys down together. Instead, first press `Ctrl-b` simultaneously, release those keys, and then immediately press the key for the command you want to send to tmux.

Throughout the rest of this book, I'll use the notation `Prefix`, followed by the shortcut key for tmux commands, like `Prefix` `d` for detaching from a session. In Chapter 2, *Configuring tmux*, on page 15, you'll remap the prefix to an easier combination, but until then, you'll use the default of `Ctrl-b` whenever you see `Prefix`.

Press the `Enter` key to dismiss the clock, and exit tmux by typing exit. Now let's look at how to run programs in the background.

Detaching and Attaching Sessions

One of tmux's biggest advantages is that you can fire it up, start up programs or processes inside the tmux environment, and then leave everything running in the background by "detaching" from the session.

If you close a regular terminal session, all the programs you have running in that session are killed off. But when you detach from a tmux session, you're not actually closing tmux. Any programs you started up in that session will stay running. You can then "attach" to the session and pick up where you left off. To demonstrate, let's create a new named tmux session, start up a program, and detach from the session. First, create the session:

```
$ tmux new -s basic
```

Then, within the tmux session, start an application called top, which monitors our memory and CPU usage, like this:

```
$ top
```

You'll have something that looks like the following figure running in your terminal.

```
top - 03:12:32 up 30 days,  7:03,  1 user,  load average: 0.00, 0.00, 0.00
Tasks: 119 total,    1 running, 118 sleeping,   0 stopped,   0 zombie
%Cpu(s):  0.0 us,  0.0 sy,  0.0 ni,100.0 id,  0.0 wa,  0.0 hi,  0.0 si,  0.0 st
KiB Mem :   500232 total,    66384 free,    47668 used,   386180 buff/cache
KiB Swap:        0 total,        0 free,        0 used.   423080 avail Mem

  PID USER      PR  NI    VIRT    RES    SHR S %CPU %MEM     TIME+ COMMAND
    1 root      20   0   37840   5124   3216 S  0.0  1.0   0:44.90 systemd
    2 root      20   0       0      0      0 S  0.0  0.0   0:00.06 kthreadd
    3 root      20   0       0      0      0 S  0.0  0.0   0:19.79 ksoftirqd/0
    5 root       0 -20       0      0      0 S  0.0  0.0   0:00.00 kworker/0:0H
    7 root      20   0       0      0      0 S  0.0  0.0   1:24.25 rcu_sched
    8 root      20   0       0      0      0 S  0.0  0.0   0:00.00 rcu_bh
    9 root      rt   0       0      0      0 S  0.0  0.0   0:00.00 migration/0
   10 root      rt   0       0      0      0 S  0.0  0.0   0:28.17 watchdog/0
   11 root      20   0       0      0      0 S  0.0  0.0   0:00.00 kdevtmpfs
   12 root       0 -20       0      0      0 S  0.0  0.0   0:00.00 netns
   13 root       0 -20       0      0      0 S  0.0  0.0   0:00.00 perf
   14 root      20   0       0      0      0 S  0.0  0.0   0:01.26 khungtaskd
   15 root       0 -20       0      0      0 S  0.0  0.0   0:00.00 writeback
   16 root      25   5       0      0      0 S  0.0  0.0   0:00.00 ksmd
   17 root       0 -20       0      0      0 S  0.0  0.0   0:00.00 crypto
[basic] 0:top*                                          "puzzles" 03:12 28-Oct-16
```

Now, detach from the tmux session by pressing Prefix d. This returns you to your regular terminal prompt.

Now, let's look at how to get back in to that tmux session we left running. But before we do, close your terminal window.

Reattaching to Existing Sessions

We've set up a tmux session, fired up a program inside the session, detached from it, and closed our terminal session, but the tmux session is still chugging along, along with the top application we launched.

You can list existing tmux sessions using the command

```
$ tmux list-sessions
```

in a new terminal window. You can shorten the command to this:

```
$ tmux ls
```

The command shows that there's one session currently running:

```
basic: 1 windows (created Tue Aug 23 16:58:26 2016) [105x25]
```

To attach to the session, use the attach keyword. If you only have one session running, you can simply use

```
$ tmux attach
```

and you'll be attached to the session again. Things get more tricky if you have more than one session running. Detach from the basic session with Prefix d.

Now create a new tmux session in the background using the command

```
$ tmux new -s second_session -d
```

This creates a new session, but doesn't attach to the session automatically.

Now list the sections, and you'll see two sessions running:

```
$ tmux ls
basic: 1 windows (created Tue Aug 23 16:58:26 2016) [105x25]
second_session: 1 windows (created Tue Aug 23 17:49:21 2016) [105x25]
```

You can attach to the session you want by using the -t flag, followed by the session name. Run the following command:

```
$ tmux attach -t second_session
```

This attaches you to the second_session tmux session. You can detach from this session just as you did previously, using Prefix d, and then attach to a different session. In *Moving Between Sessions*, on page 66, you'll see some other ways to move between active sessions. But for now, let's remove the active sessions.

Killing Sessions

You can type exit within a session to destroy the session, but you can also kill off sessions with the kill-session command. It works just like tmux attach:

```
$ tmux kill-session -t basic
$ tmux kill-session -t second_session
```

This is useful for situations where a program in a session is hanging.

If you list the sessions again, you'll get this message:

```
$ tmux ls
no server running on /tmp/tmux-1002/default
```

Since there are no tmux sessions running, tmux itself isn't running, so it isn't able to handle the request.

Now that you know the basics of creating and working with sessions, let's look at how we can work with multiple programs within a single session.

Working with Windows

It's possible, and very common, to run multiple, simultaneous commands within a tmux session. We can keep these organized with windows, which are similar to tabs in modern graphical terminal emulators or web browsers.

When we create a new tmux session, the environment sets up an initial window for us. We can create as many as we'd like, and they will persist when we detach and reattach.

Let's create a new session that has two windows. The first window will have our normal prompt, and the second window will run the top command. Create a named session called "windows," like this:

```
$ tmux new -s windows -n shell
```

By using the -n flag, we tell tmux to name the first window so we can identify it easily.

Now let's add a window to this session.

Creating and Naming Windows

To create a window in a current session, press `Prefix` `c`. Creating a window like this automatically brings the new window into focus. From here, you can start up another application. Let's start top in this new window.

```
$ top
```

The first window has a name you defined, called "shell," but the second window now appears to have the name "top." This window's name changes based on the app that's currently running because you never gave it a default name when you created it. So let's give this window a proper name.

To rename a window, press `Prefix` followed by `,` (a comma), and the status line changes, letting you rename the current window. Go ahead and rename the window to "Processes."

You can create as many windows in a tmux session as you'd like. But once you have more than one, you need to be able to move between them.

Moving Between Windows

So far, you've created two windows in your environment, and you can navigate around these windows in several ways. When you only have two windows, you can quickly move between windows with `Prefix n`, for "next window." This cycles through the windows you have open. Since you only have two windows right now, this just toggles between them.

You can use `Prefix p` to go to the *previous* window.

By default, windows in tmux each have a number, starting at 0. You can quickly jump to the first window with `Prefix 0`, and the second window with `Prefix 1`. This zero-based array of windows isn't always intuitive, and in Chapter 2, *Configuring tmux*, on page 15, you'll see how to make the list of windows start at one instead of zero.

If you end up with more than nine windows, you can use `Prefix w` to display a visual menu of your windows so you can select the one you'd like. You can also use `Prefix f` to find a window that contains a string of text. Typing the text and pressing `Enter` displays a list of windows containing that text.

From here, you can continue creating new windows and launching programs. When you detach from your session and reattach later, your windows will all be where you left them.

To close a window, you can either type "exit" into the prompt in the window, or you can use `Prefix &`, which displays a confirmation message in the status bar before killing off the window. If you accept, your previous window comes into focus. To completely close out the tmux session, you have to close all the windows in the session.

Creating windows is great, but we can make tmux even more useful by splitting a window into panes.

Working with Panes

Having programs in separate windows is fine for stuff we don't mind having out of the way. But with tmux, we can divide a single session into panes.

Create a new tmux session called "panes" so we can experiment with how panes work. Exit any existing tmux sessions and create a new one like this:

```
$ tmux new -s panes
```

We can split windows vertically or horizontally. Let's split the window in half vertically first, and then horizontally, creating one large pane on the left and two smaller panes on the right, as shown in the figure on page 10.

In the tmux session, press `Prefix %`, and the window will divide down the middle and start up a second terminal session in the new pane. In addition, the focus will move to this new pane. Pressing `Prefix "` (double quote) will split

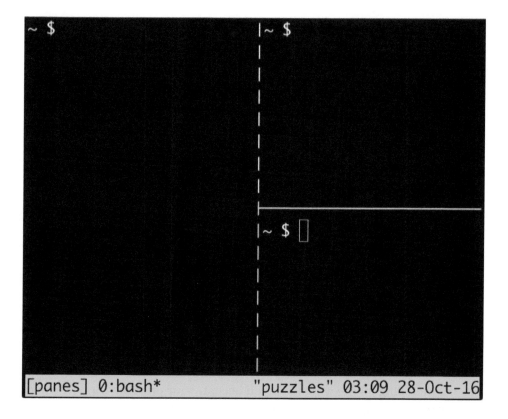

```
~ $                          |~ $
                             |
                             |
                             |
                             |
                             |
                             |
                             |
                             |
                             |------------------------------
                             |~ $ []
                             |
                             |
                             |
                             |
                             |
                             |
                             |
[panes] 0:bash*              "puzzles" 03:09 28-Oct-16
```

this new pane in half horizontally. By default, new panes split the existing pane in half evenly.

To cycle through the panes, press `Prefix` `o`. You can also use `Prefix`, followed by the `Up`, `Down`, `Left`, or `Right` keys to move around the panes.

With just a couple keystrokes, we've divided one window into a workspace with three panes. Let's look at how we can rearrange these panes with layouts.

Pane Layouts

We can resize a pane, either using incremental resizing or by using templates. Resizing panes incrementally using the default keybindings is quite awkward. In Chapter 2, *Configuring tmux*, on page 15, we'll define some shortcuts to make resizing panes easier. For now, we'll use one of tmux's several default pane layouts:

- even-horizontal stacks all panes horizontally, left to right.

- even-vertical stacks all panes vertically, top to bottom.

- main-horizontal creates one larger pane on the top and smaller panes underneath.

- main-vertical creates one large pane on the left side of the screen, and stacks the rest of the panes vertically on the right.

- tiled arranges all panes evenly on the screen.

You can cycle through these layouts by pressing `Prefix` `Spacebar`.

Closing Panes

You close a pane the same way you exit a terminal session or a tmux window: you simply type "exit" in the pane. You can also kill a pane with `Prefix` `x`, which also closes the window if there's only one pane in that window.

You'll be asked to confirm if you want to kill the specified pane. Killing a pane like this is great for situations where the pane has gotten stuck, or you can't interact with it anymore.

So far, we've been able to create new sessions, create windows and panes, and move around a bit. Before we move on to more advanced topics, let's explore some additional tmux commands.

Working with Command Mode

So far, we've used key combinations to create windows and panes, but those keybindings are actually just shortcuts for tmux commands with some preset options. We can execute tmux commands two ways: from the terminal itself or from the command area in the tmux status line. You'll learn about using tmux commands from the terminal in Chapter 3, *Scripting Customized tmux Environments*, on page 35, but for now, let's explore tmux's Command mode by using it to create some new windows and panes in our workspace.

To enter Command mode, press `Prefix` `:` (the colon) from within a running tmux session. The status line changes color and we get a prompt that indicates that we can type our command. Create a new window by using the new-window command, like this:

```
new-window -n console
```

By using a command rather than the shortcut, you can create a new window and give it a name at the same time by using the -n flag. Let's take this a step further and launch a new window that starts the top program. To do that, we enter Command mode and type this command:

```
new-window -n processes "top"
```

When you press Enter, a new window appears and the top application runs, showing your running processes.

Specifying an initial command for a window is extremely handy for short-term tasks, but there's a slight wrinkle; if you exit the top app by pressing q, the tmux window you created will also close. You can use configuration settings to get around this, but if you want the window to persist, simply create it without specifying an initial command, and then execute your own command in the new window.

You can use Command mode to create new windows, new panes, or new sessions, or even set other environmental options. In Chapter 2, *Configuring tmux*, on page 15, we'll create a few custom keybindings to make some of these commands easier to use.

What's Next?

In this chapter, you explored the very basic usage of tmux sessions, panes, windows, and commands, but there's a lot more you can try.

By pressing Prefix ?, you can get a list of all predefined tmux keybindings and the associated commands these trigger.

As you work with tmux, think about how you can create different environments for your work. If you're monitoring servers, you could use tmux panes to create a dashboard that shows your various monitoring scripts and log files.

With the basics under our belt, let's put together a custom configuration we can use for the rest of our work.

For Future Reference

Creating Sessions

Command	Description
tmux new-session	Creates a new session without a name. Can be shortened to tmux new or simply tmux.
tmux new -s development	Creates a new session called "development."
tmux new -s development -n editor	Creates a session named "development" and names the first window "editor."
tmux attach -t development	Attaches to a session named "development."

Default Commands for Sessions, Windows, and Panes

Command	Description
Prefix d	Detaches from the session, leaving the session running in the background.
Prefix :	Enters Command mode.
Prefix c	Creates a new window from within an existing tmux session. Shortcut for new-window.
Prefix n	Moves to the next window.
Prefix p	Moves to the previous window.
Prefix 0...9	Selects windows by number.
Prefix w	Displays a selectable list of windows in the current session.
Prefix f	Searches for a window that contains the text you specify. Displays a selectable list of windows containing that text in the current session.
Prefix ,	Displays a prompt to rename a window.
Prefix &	Closes the current window after prompting for confirmation.
Prefix %	Divides the current window in half vertically.
Prefix "	Divides the current window in half horizontally.
Prefix o	Cycles through open panes.
Prefix q	Momentarily displays pane numbers in each pane.
Prefix x	Closes the current pane after prompting for confirmation.
Prefix Space	Cycles through the various pane layouts.

## CHAPTER 2

Configuring tmux

tmux, by default, doesn't have the most friendly commands. Many of the most important and useful features are assigned to hard-to-reach keystrokes or consist of long, verbose command strings. And tmux's default color scheme isn't very easy on the eyes. In this chapter, you'll build a basic configuration file for your environment that you'll then use for the rest of this book. You'll start out by customizing how you navigate around the screen and how you create and resize panes, and then you'll explore some more advanced settings. You'll also learn how to make sure your terminal is properly configured so that some of the settings you'll make to tmux's appearance look good on your screen. When you're done, you'll have a better understanding of how flexible tmux is, and you can start making it your own. Let's start by talking about how to configure tmux in the first place.

Introducing the .tmux.conf File

By default, tmux looks for configuration settings in two places. It first looks in /etc/tmux.conf for a system-wide configuration. It then looks for a file called .tmux.conf in the current user's home directory. If these files don't exist, tmux simply uses its default settings. We don't need to create a system-wide configuration, so let's create a brand-new configuration file in our home directory. Execute the following command in your shell:

```
$ touch ~/.tmux.conf
```

In this file we can do everything from defining new key shortcuts to setting up a default environment with multiple windows, panes, and running programs. Let's start by setting a couple basic options that will make working with tmux much easier.

The .tmux.conf file is a hidden file and doesn't show up in file explorers or directory listings by default. The labels above the code listings in this book reference the file as tmux.conf, without the leading period, so it corresponds with the file in the book's source code download.

Defining an Easier Prefix

As you saw earlier, tmux uses `Ctrl-b` as its command prefix. Many tmux users started out using GNU-Screen, which uses `Ctrl-a` for its command prefix. `Ctrl-a` is an excellent choice for a prefix because it's easier to trigger, especially if you remap your computer's `Caps Lock` key to `Ctrl` as explained in the sidebar that follows. This keeps your hands on the home row of your keyboard.

To set options in the .tmux.conf file, use the set-option command, which you can shorten to set. You define the tmux prefix by adding this to the .tmux.conf file:

config/tmux.conf
```
# Setting the prefix from C-b to C-a
set -g prefix C-a
```

In this example, we're using the -g switch, for "global," which sets the option for all tmux sessions we create.

The line starting with # is a comment. It's a good idea to put comments in your configuration files; they'll jog your memory later on when you go back and look at your configuration a few months from now. Comments in a tmux configuration file work just like comments in source code.

While not necessary, we can use the unbind-key, or unbind command, to remove a keybinding that's been defined, so we can assign a different command to this key later. Let's free up `Ctrl-b` like this:

config/tmux.conf
```
# Free the original Ctrl-b prefix keybinding
unbind C-b
```

Changes to the file aren't read by tmux automatically. So if you're editing your .tmux.conf file while tmux is running, you'll either need to completely close *all* tmux sessions, or enter tmux's Command mode with `Prefix` `:` and type this whenever you make a change:

```
source-file ~/.tmux.conf
```

You can now use `Ctrl-a` for your prefix. The rest of the examples in this book will continue to refer to it as `Prefix`, though.

> ## Remapping the Caps Lock Key
>
> On many keyboards, the `Caps Lock` key sits right next to the `a` key on the home row of the keyboard. By remapping this key to `Ctrl`, you can make triggering commands more comfortable.
>
> On your Mac, you can remap the `Caps Lock` key under the Keyboard preference pane, under System Preferences. Just press the Modifier Keys button and change the action for `Caps Lock` to "Control."
>
> Under Linux, the process can be a little more tricky depending on your distribution or window manager, but you can find several methods described on the Emacs wiki.[a]
>
> This small change to your configuration can save you a surprising amount of time over the course of a day.
>
> _____
>
> a. http://www.emacswiki.org/emacs/MovingTheCtrlKey

Changing the Default Delay

tmux adds a very small delay when sending commands, and this delay can interfere with other programs such as the Vim text editor. We can set this delay so it's much more responsive. Add this line to your configuration file:

```
#setting the delay between prefix and command
set -s escape-time 1
```

Once you reload the configuration file, you'll be able to issue keystrokes without delay.

Setting the Window and Panes Index

In Chapter 1, *Learning the Basics*, on page 1, you learned about windows and how when you create more than one window in a session, you have to reference windows by their index. This index starts at zero, which can be a little awkward, since you'd have to use `Prefix 0` to access the first window. By adding this line to your configuration file

```
# Set the base index for windows to 1 instead of 0
set -g base-index 1
```

the window index will start at 1, so you can use `Prefix 1` to jump to the first window. That's a lot easier since the keys on the keyboard now directly correspond with the windows listed in the status line.

You can also set the starting index for panes using the `pane-base-index` option. Add this line to your configuration so you have some consistency between pane and window numbering.

```
config/tmux.conf
# Set the base index for panes to 1 instead of 0
setw -g pane-base-index 1
```

Up until now, we've used the set command, which sets options for the tmux session. In order to configure options that affect how we interact with windows, we have to use another command, called set-window-option, which we can shorten to setw. In this book, I've used the shortened versions of commands to make the configuration examples fit on one line.

Now let's build some useful shortcuts that will increase your productivity.

Customizing Keys, Commands, and User Input

Many of the default keyboard shortcuts in tmux are a bit of a stretch, both physically and mentally. Not only is `Prefix` `%` hard to press, as it involves holding three keys, but without looking at the command reference, there's no easy way to remember what it does.

In this section, we'll define, or redefine, some of the most-used tmux commands. Let's start by creating a custom keybinding to reload the tmux configuration.

Creating a Shortcut to Reload the Configuration

Every time you make a change to your configuration file, you either have to shut down *all* sessions and then restart tmux, or issue the source command to reload your configuration from within the running instances. Let's create a custom keybinding to reload the configuration file.

The bind command defines a new keybinding. You specify the key you want to use, followed by the command you want to perform.

Let's define `Prefix` `r` so it reloads the .tmux.conf file in the current session. Add this line to your configuration file:

```
bind r source-file ~/.tmux.conf
```

When you define keybindings using bind, you still have to push the `Prefix` key before you can press the newly defined key. And while you just defined a new command to make reloading the tmux configuration easier, you can't use it until you reload the configuration file. So be sure to enter Command mode with `Prefix` `:` and type

```
source-file ~/.tmux.conf
```

one more time.

When you reload the file, you might not always be able to tell that anything changed, but you can use the display command to put a message in the status line. Modify your reload command to display the text "Reloaded!" when the configuration file loads:

config/tmux.conf
```
# Reload the file with Prefix r
bind r source-file ~/.tmux.conf \; display "Reloaded!"
```

As you can see, you can bind a key to a series of commands by separating the commands with the \; character combination.

> ### Defining Keybindings That Don't Require a Prefix
>
> Using the bind command with the -n prefix tells tmux that the keybinding doesn't require pressing the prefix. For example,
>
> ```
> bind-key -n C-r source-file ~/.tmux.conf
> ```
>
> would make Ctrl-r reload the configuration file. Unfortunately, this would completely disable that key combination in any application that's running in a tmux session, so you'll want to use this with care.

With this keybinding in place, you can make additional changes to the configuration file and then immediately activate them by pressing Prefix r.

Sending the Prefix to Other Applications

We've remapped Ctrl-a as the Prefix, but programs such as Vim, Emacs, and even the regular Bash shell also use that combination. You'll probably want to configure tmux to send that command through when you need it. You can do that by binding the send-prefix command to a keystroke, like this:

```
# Ensure that we can send Ctrl-A to other apps
bind C-a send-prefix
```

After reloading the configuration file, you can send Ctrl-a to an application running within tmux simply by pressing Ctrl-a twice.

Splitting Panes

The default keys for splitting panes can be difficult to remember, so let's set our own keys that we won't be able to forget. We'll set the horizontal split to Prefix | and the vertical split to Prefix -. To do that, add these lines to your configuration:

```
config/tmux.conf
# splitting panes with | and -
bind | split-window -h
bind - split-window -v
```

At first glance, this may look backwards. The -v and -h flags on split-window stand for "vertical" and "horizontal" splits, but to tmux, a vertical split means creating a new pane below the existing pane so the panes are stacked vertically on top of each other. A horizontal split means creating a new pane *next* to the existing one so the panes are stacked horizontally across the screen. So, in order to divide the window vertically, we use a "horizontal" split, and to divide it horizontally, we use a "vertical" split.

These new shortcuts give us a nice visual association. If we want our windows split, we simply press the key that looks like the split we want to create.

Remapping Movement Keys

Moving from pane to pane with `Prefix` `o` is cumbersome, and using the arrow keys means you have to take your fingers off the home row. If you use the Vim text editor, you're probably familiar with its use of `h`, `j`, `k`, and `l` for movement keys. You can remap the movement keys in tmux to these same keys.

```
# moving between panes with Prefix h,j,k,l
bind h select-pane -L
bind j select-pane -D
bind k select-pane -U
bind l select-pane -R
```

In addition, you can use `Prefix` `Ctrl-h` and `Prefix` `Ctrl-l` to cycle through the windows by binding those keystrokes to the respective commands:

```
# Quick window selection
bind -r C-h select-window -t :-
bind -r C-l select-window -t :+
```

Provided you've mapped your `Caps Lock` key to the `Ctrl` key, you can now move between panes without moving your hands off the home row.

Resizing Panes

To resize a pane, you can enter Command mode and type resize-pane -D to resize a pane downward one row at a time. You can increase the resizing increment by passing a number after the direction, such as resize-pane -D 5. The command itself is pretty verbose, but you can make some keybindings to make resizing panes easier.

Let's use a variation of the Vim movement keys to resize windows. We'll use Prefix H, Prefix J, Prefix K, and Prefix L to change the size of the panes. Add these lines to your configuration file:

```
bind H resize-pane -L 5
bind J resize-pane -D 5
bind K resize-pane -U 5
bind L resize-pane -R 5
```

Notice that we're using uppercase letters in the configuration file. tmux allows both lowercase and uppercase letters for keystrokes. You'll need to use the Shift key to trigger the uppercase keystroke.

Using these movement keys will help us keep track of which way we want the window size to change. For example, if we have a window divided into two panes stacked vertically, like this

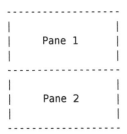

and we want to increase the size of Pane 1, then we'd place our cursor inside Pane 1 and then press Prefix J, which moves the horizontal divider *downward*. If we pressed Prefix K, we would move the horizontal divider up.

With the configuration we just used, you have to use the Prefix each time you want to resize the pane. But if you use the -r flag with the bind command, you can specify that you want the key to be *repeatable*, meaning you can press the prefix key only once and then continuously press the defined key within a given window of time, called the repeat limit.

Redefine the window resizing commands by adding the -r option:

```
# Pane resizing panes with Prefix H,J,K,L
bind -r H resize-pane -L 5
bind -r J resize-pane -D 5
bind -r K resize-pane -U 5
bind -r L resize-pane -R 5
```

Now you can resize the panes by pressing Prefix J once, and then press J until the window is the size you want. The default repeat limit is 500 milliseconds, and can be changed by setting the repeat-time option to a higher value.

Now let's turn our attention to how tmux can work with the mouse.

Handling the Mouse

While tmux is meant to be completely keyboard-driven, there are times when you may find it easier to use the mouse. If your terminal is set up to forward mouse clicks and movement through to programs in the terminal, then you can tell tmux how to handle certain mouse events.

Sometimes it's nice to be able to scroll up through the terminal buffer with the mouse wheel, or to select windows and panes, especially when you're just getting started with tmux. To configure tmux so we can use the mouse, we need to enable mouse mode.

```
set -g mouse on
```

This setting configures tmux so it will let us use the mouse to select a pane or resize a pane, let us click the window list to select a window, or even let us use the mouse to scroll backwards through the buffer if your terminal supports it.

This can be a handy addition to your configuration, but remember that using the mouse with tmux will slow you down. Even though being able to scroll and click might seem like a neat idea, you should learn the keyboard equivalents for switching panes and moving forward and backward through the buffers. So, for our configuration file, we're going to disable the mouse.

config/tmux.conf
```
# mouse support - set to on if you want to use the mouse
set -g mouse off
```

Setting this option prevents us from accidentally doing things when we select the terminal window with our mouse, and it forces us to get more comfortable with the keyboard.

The flexible configuration system tmux provides lets you customize the way you interact with the interface, but you can also configure its appearance to make its interface easier to see, and in some cases, more informative.

Visual Styling

tmux provides quite a few ways to customize your environment's appearance. In this section, we'll walk through configuring some of these options, as we customize the status line and other components. We'll start by configuring the colors for various elements, then we'll turn our bland status line into something that will provide us with some vital information about our environment.

Configuring Colors

To get the best visual experience out of tmux, make sure that both your terminal and tmux are configured for 256 colors.

Using the tput command, you can quickly determine the number of colors supported by your terminal session. Enter the command

```
$ tput colors
256
```

into your terminal. If you don't see 256 as the result, you'll need to do a little configuration.

You may need to configure your terminal to use xterm's 256 mode. On the Mac, you can configure this in the Terminal app by editing the profile as shown in the following figure:

If you're using iTerm2,[1] you can find this by editing the default profile and changing the terminal mode to xterm-256color, as shown in the following figure:

---

1. http://www.iterm2.com

If you're using Linux, you might need to add

```
[ -z "$TMUX" ] && export TERM=xterm-256color
```

to your .bashrc file to enable a 256-color terminal. This conditional statement ensures that the TERM variable is only set outside of tmux, since tmux sets its own terminal.

Also, ensure that your terminal emulator supports displaying UTF-8 characters so that visual elements such as the pane dividers appear as dashed lines.

To make tmux display things in 256 colors, add this line to our .tmux.conf file:

config/tmux.conf
```
# Set the default terminal mode to 256color mode
set -g default-terminal "screen-256color"
```

Once the right color mode is set, you'll find it much easier to use programs such as Vim, Emacs, and other full-color programs from within tmux, especially when you are using more complex color schemes for syntax highlighting. Just take a look at this figure to see the difference.

Now let's configure the appearance of tmux's components, starting with colors.

Changing Colors

You can change the colors of several parts of the tmux interface, including the status line, window list, message area, and even the pane borders.

tmux provides variables you can use to specify colors, including black, red, green, yellow, blue, magenta, cyan, or white. You can also use colour0 to colour255 to reference more specific colors on the 256 color palette.

To find the numbers for those colors, you can run this simple shell script to get the color variable you'd like to use:[2]

```
for i in {0..255} ; do
  printf "\x1b[38;5;${i}m${i} "
done
```

---

2.   http://superuser.com/questions/285381/how-does-the-tmux-color-palette-work

When you execute this command, you'll see the following output in your terminal, displaying the colors:

tmux has specific configuration options to change foreground and background colors for each of its components. Let's start exploring these by customizing the colors of the status line.

Changing the Status Line Colors

The default status line has black text on a bright green background. It's pretty bland, and depending on your terminal configuration, it can be hard to read. Let's make it have white text on a black background by default, so it looks like this:

```
[0] 1:bash*                                    "puzzles" 03:57 31-Oct-16
```

The status-style option sets the foreground and background colors of the status line, as well as the style. Add the following line to your configuration to set the status line colors:

config/tmux.conf
```
# set the status line's colors
set -g status-style fg=white,bg=black
```

You can set the foreground color and the background color, and you can control the appearance of the text, depending on whether or not your terminal supports it. As you can probably guess, the fg option sets the foreground color, and the bg option sets the background color.

This command supports the options dim, bright (or bold), reverse, and blink in addition to colors. For example, to make the status line's text white and bold, you'd use the following configuration:

```
set -g status-style fg=white,bold,bg=black
```

You can also customize the colors of the items within the status line. Let's start by customizing the window list.

Changing the Window List Colors

tmux displays a list of windows in the status line. Let's make it more apparent which window is active by styling the active window red and the inactive windows cyan. The option window-status-style controls how regular windows look, and the window-status-current-style option controls how the active window looks. To configure the colors, you use the same syntax you used for the status-style option.

Let's make the names of the windows cyan, like this:

```
[0] 1:bash*                                "puzzles" 04:02 31-Oct-16
```

Add this to your configuration file:

config/tmux.conf
```
# set the color of the window list
setw -g window-status-style fg=cyan,bg=black
```

You can use default for a value so it inherits from the color of the status line.

To style the active window with a red background and bold white text, add this to your configuration:

```
# set colors for the active window
setw -g window-status-current-style fg=white,bold,bg=red
```

Now inactive windows are cyan, and the active window is easily identifiable:

```
[0] 1:bash- 2:bash*                        "puzzles" 04:06 31-Oct-16
```

This takes care of the window list. Let's look at how we can customize how panes within a window appear.

Changing the Appearance of Panes

We have a few options to control how panes look. We can control the color of the pane dividers, we can define colors to make the active pane more apparent, and we can even "dim out" the inactive panes.

Panes have both foreground and background colors. The foreground color of a pane is the actual dashed line that makes up the border. The background color, by default, is black, but if we color it when the pane is active, we can make the active pane extremely noticeable, as shown in the following figure:

Add this to your configuration file to add this effect to your environment:

config/tmux.conf
```
# colors for pane borders
setw -g pane-border-style fg=green,bg=black
setw -g pane-active-border-style fg=white,bg=yellow
```

Finally, you may want to be able to more easily determine what the active pane is by changing the color of the foreground or background of the current pane. Or, you might want to fade out panes that are not in use. The set-window-style and set-window-active-style options let you control the foreground and background colors, although you have to specify both the foreground and background colors as part of the value you set for the option.

Let's dim out any pane that's not active. We'll achieve this by actually dimming all of the panes, and then making the active pane look normal. Add these lines to your configuration:

```
# active pane normal, other shaded out
setw -g window-style fg=colour240,bg=colour235
setw -g window-active-style fg=white,bg=black
```

To create the dimming effect, we set the foreground text color to a lighter grey, and then use a darker grey for the background color. Then for the active window, we use black and white.

With this change and the active pane borders, it should be pretty clear which pane is active. Now let's touch up the area of tmux where we issue commands.

Customizing the tmux Command Line

We can also customize the command line, where we enter tmux commands and see alert messages. The approach is almost identical to the way we styled the status line itself. Let's change the background color to black and the text color to white. We'll use a bright white so the message stands out in more detail. Add this to your configuration:

config/tmux.conf
```
# Command / message line
set -g message-style fg=white,bold,bg=black
```

That was easy. Now let's change the areas of the status line on both sides of the window list.

Customizing the Status Line's Content

The tmux status line can display nearly any information we want. We can use some predefined components or create our own by executing shell commands.

The status line consists of three components: a left panel, the window list, and a right panel. By default, it looks like this:

```
[development] 0:bash*                          "example.local" 13:37 31-Oct-16
```

On the left side, we have the name of the tmux session followed by the list of windows. The list of windows shows the numerical index of the current window and its name. On the right side, we have the hostname of our server followed by the date and time. Let's customize the content of our status line.

Configuring Status Line Items

You can change the content in the left or right panels of the status bar using a combination of text and variables. The following table shows the possible variables we can use in our status line.

Variable	Description
#H	Hostname of local host
#h	Hostname of local host without the domain name
#F	Current window flag
#I	Current window index
#P	Current pane index
#S	Current session name
#T	Current window title
#W	Current window name

Variable	Description
##	A literal #
#(shell-command)	First line of the shell command's output
#[attributes]	Color or attribute change

Table 1—Status Line Variables

For example, if you wanted to show just the name of the current tmux session on the left, you'd use the set-option -g status-left option with the #S value, like this:

```
set -g status-left "#S"
```

But you can also make it stand out more by using an attribute to set the foreground color, like this:

```
set -g status-left "#[fg=green]#S"
```

You can add as many attributes and items to the status line as you want. To demonstrate, let's alter the left side of the status line so it shows the session name in green, the current window number in yellow, and the current pane in cyan. Add this line to your configuration file:

```
set -g status-left "#[fg=green]#S #[fg=yellow]#I #[fg=cyan]#P"
```

You can add any arbitrary text into the status line, too. Let's add text to make the session, window, and pane more noticeable, like this:

```
config/tmux.conf
# Status line left side to show Session:window:pane
set -g status-left-length 40
set -g status-left "#[fg=green]Session: #S #[fg=yellow]#I #[fg=cyan]#P"
```

We set the status-left-length option because the output we've specified is too long for the default length, so we have to make that region wider.

You can configure the right side of the status line too. Add the current date and time, like this:

```
config/tmux.conf
# Status line right side -  31-Oct 13:37
set -g status-right "#[fg=cyan]%d %b %R"
```

This formats the date as "31-Oct 13:37," but you can format it however you'd like, using the standard strftime() time formatting mechanism used in many programming languages.[3] Your status line should now look like this:

```
Session: 0 2 11:bash- 2:bash*                          31 Oct 04:25
```

---

3. See http://www.foragoodstrftime.com/ for a handy tool to help you find the perfect time format.

You can take things a step further by incorporating shell commands into the mix by using the #(shell-command) variable to return the result of any external command-line program into the status line. We'll go into this in detail in *Adding Battery Life to the Status Line*, on page 71.

Keeping Status Line Info Up to Date

We've added the current time and some other dynamic information to our status line, but we need to tell tmux how often to refresh that information periodically. By default, tmux refreshes the status line every 15 seconds. We can specify exactly how quickly tmux refreshes its status line with set-option -g status-interval followed by the refresh interval in seconds, like this:

```
# Update the status line every sixty seconds
set -g status-interval 60
```

This would refresh the status line every 60 seconds. Keep in mind that if you're firing off shell commands, those will be executed once per interval, so be careful not to load too many resource-intensive scripts.

Centering the Window List

We can also control the placement of the window list. By default, the window list is left-aligned, but we can center the window list in between the left and right status areas with a single configuration change:

config/tmux.conf
```
# Center the window list in the status line
set -g status-justify centre
```

With this in place, the window list appears centered:

```
Session: 0 2 1          1:bash- 2:bash*              31 Oct 04:26
```

As you create new windows, the window list will shift accordingly, staying in the center of the status line.

Identifying Activity in Other Windows

When you're working with more than one window, you'll want to be notified when something happens in one of the other windows in your session so you can react to it. You can do that by adding a visual notification, like this:

config/tmux.conf
```
# enable activity alerts
setw -g monitor-activity on
set -g visual-activity on
```

The monitor-activity on command highlights the window name in the status line when there's activity in that window. The visual-activity on line tells tmux to show a message in the status line as well.

Now when one of the other windows has some activity, it'll stand out with a cyan background, like the "top" window shown here:

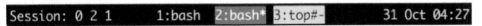

Once you switch to that window, the colors will revert back to normal. If you want to configure different colors, you can do so with setw -g window-status-activity-style and the colors of your choice.

What's Next?

We've built up a pretty solid configuration file throughout this chapter. Look at Appendix 1, *Our Configuration*, on page 77 to see the whole .tmux.conf file.

You can define additional options in your .tmux.conf file. For example, in Chapter 3, *Scripting Customized tmux Environments*, on page 35, you'll set up a custom default work environment using project-specific configuration files.

In addition, you can configure a default configuration for your system in /etc/tmux.conf. This is great for situations where you've set up a shared server so members of your team can collaborate, or if you just want to ensure that every user on the system has some sensible defaults.

Now that you have a configuration defined, let's look at creating your own custom development environments with scripts so you can take advantage of tmux's panes and windows without having to set them up every day.

For Future Reference

Keybindings defined in this chapter

Command	Description
Ctrl-a	The new Prefix.
Prefix a	Sends Ctrl-a to the program running in a tmux window or pane.
Prefix r	Reloads the tmux configuration file.
Prefix |	Splits the window horizontally.
Prefix -	Splits the window vertically.

Command	Description
`Prefix` `h`, `Prefix` `j`, `Prefix` `k`, and `Prefix` `l`	Moves between panes.
`Prefix` `H`, `Prefix` `J`, `Prefix` `K`, and `Prefix` `L`	Resizes the current pane.
`Prefix` `Ctrl`-`h` and `Prefix` `Ctrl`-`l`	Moves forward and backward through windows.

Commands to control tmux's behavior

Command	Description
`set -g prefix C-a`	Sets the key combination for the Prefix key.
`set -sg escape-time n`	Sets the amount of time (in milliseconds) tmux waits for a keystroke after pressing `Prefix`.
`set -g base-index 1`	Sets the base index for windows to 1 instead of 0.
`setw -g pane-base-index 1`	Sets the base index for panes to 1 instead of 0.
`source-file [file]`	Loads a configuration file. Use this to reload the existing configuration or bring in additional configuration options later.
`bind C-a send-prefix`	Configures tmux to send the prefix when pressing the `Prefix` combination twice consecutively.
`bind-key [key] [command]`	Creates a keybinding that executes the specified command. Can be shortened to `bind`.
`bind-key -r [key] [command]`	Creates a keybinding that is repeatable, meaning you only need to press the `Prefix` key once, and you can press the assigned key repeatedly afterwards. This is useful for commands where you want to cycle through elements or resize panes. Can be shortened to `bind`.
`unbind-key [key]`	Removes a defined keybinding so it can be bound to a different command. Can be shortened to `unbind`.
`display-message or display`	Displays the given text in the status message.
`set-option [flags] [option] [value]`	Sets options for sessions. Using the `-g` flag sets the option for all sessions.
`set-window-option [option] [value]`	Sets options for windows, such as activity notifications, cursor movement, or other elements related to windows and panes.
`set -a`	Appends values onto existing options rather than replacing the option's value.

Command	Description
set -g mouse off	Disables mouse support in tmux. Set to on if you wish to use the mouse.
set -g default-terminal "screen-256color"	Defines the terminal type for windows. Sets the value of TERM, which other programs will use. screen-256color ensures the widest compatibility with programs originally written for the screen program.

Commands to control tmux's appearance

Command	Description
set -g status-style	Sets the foreground and background color for the status line. Supports the options dim, bright (or bold), reverse, and blink in addition to colors.
	Example: set -g status-style fg=white,bold,bg=black
setw -g window-status-style	Sets the foreground and background color of the window list in the status line. Uses the same options as status-style.
setw -g window-status-current-style	Sets the foreground and background color of the active window in the window list in the status line. Uses the same options as status-style.
setw -g window-status-activity-style	Sets the foreground and background color of any window with background activity. Uses the same options as status-style.
setw -g pane-border-style	Sets the foreground and background color of the pane borders. Uses the same options as status-style.
setw -g pane-active-border-style	Sets the foreground and background color of the active pane's border. Uses the same options as status-style.
setw -g window-style	Sets the foreground and background color of the window. Uses the same options as status-style.
setw -g window-active-style	Sets the foreground and background color of the active window. Uses the same options as status-style.

Command	Description
setw -g message-style	Sets the foreground and background color of the message area and tmux command line. Uses the same options as status-style.
set -g status-length-left and set -g status-length-right	Controls the number of visible characters in the left and right sides of the status line.
set -g status-left and set -g status-right	Configures the items that appear in the left and right sides of the status line.
set -g status-interval n	Defines the refresh interval for the status line, where n is the number of seconds between refreshes.
set -g status-justify centre	Centers the window list in the status line.
setw -g monitor-activity on	Looks for activity in other windows and highlights the name of the window with background activity.
set -g visual-activity on	Displays a message in the message area when there is activity in another window.

## CHAPTER 3

Scripting Customized tmux Environments

You probably run a wide collection of tools and programs as you work on your projects. If you're working on a web application, you most likely need to have a command shell, a text editor, a database console, and another window dedicated to running your automated test suite for your application. That's a lot of windows to manage, and a lot of commands to type to get it all fired up.

Imagine being able to come to your workstation, ready to tackle that new feature, and being able to bring every one of those programs up, each in its own pane or window in a single tmux session, using a single command. We can use tmux's client-server model to create custom scripts that build up our development environments, splitting windows and launching programs for us automatically. We'll explore how to do this manually first, and then we'll look at more advanced automatic tools.

Creating a Custom Setup with tmux Commands

We've already explored how we use the tmux command to create new tmux sessions, but the tmux command takes many other options. We can take an existing session and split its windows into panes, change layouts, or even start up applications within the session.

The key to this is the -t switch, or the "target." When you have a named tmux session, you can attach to it like this:

```
$ tmux attach -t [session_name]
```

You can use this target switch to direct a tmux command to the appropriate tmux session. Create a new tmux session called "development," like this:

```
$ tmux new-session -s development
```

Then detach from the session with `Prefix` `d`. Even though you're no longer connected, you can split the window in the tmux session horizontally by issuing this command:

```
$ tmux split-window -h -t development
```

When you attach to the session again, the window will split into two panes. Attach to your session again to see for yourself.

```
$ tmux attach -t development
```

In fact, you don't even have to detach from a tmux session to send commands. You can open another terminal and split the window again, but this time with a vertical split. Try it out. Open a second terminal window or tab, and enter this command:

```
$ tmux split-window -v -t development
```

Using this approach, you can customize your environment easily. Let's explore this concept by creating our own development environment.

Scripting a Project Configuration

In Chapter 1, *Learning the Basics*, on page 1, we discussed tmux commands such as new-session and new-window. Let's write a simple script using these and similar commands that creates a new tmux session and creates a window with a couple panes and two additional windows with one pane each. To top it off, we'll launch applications in each of the panes.

Let's start by creating a new script called development in our home directory. We'll make this script executable too, so we can run it like any other executable program from our shell. Execute these commands in your terminal:

```
$ touch ~/development
$ chmod +x ~/development
```

When we start up our session, we want to change to the directory for our project. We'll call that directory devproject. And before we can change to that directory, we'd better create it first.

```
$ mkdir ~/devproject
```

Now, open the ~/development script in your text editor and add this line to create a new tmux session called "development":

scripting/development
```
tmux new-session -s development -n editor -d
```

We're passing a couple additional parameters when we create this new session. First, we're creating this session and naming it with the -s flag like we've done before. Then we give the initial window a name of "editor," and then immediately detach from this new session with the -d flag.

Next, add a line to our configuration that uses tmux's send-keys command to change the current directory to the one we're using for our project:

```
tmux send-keys -t development 'cd ~/devproject' C-m
```

We place C-m at the end of the line to send the Carriage Return sequence, represented by Ctrl-M.[1] This is how we tell tmux to press the Enter key.

We'll use the same approach to open the Vim text editor in that window. Add this line to your script:

```
tmux send-keys -t development 'vim' C-m
```

With these three commands, we've created a new session, changed to a directory, and opened a text editor, but our environment isn't yet complete. Let's split the main editor window so we have a small terminal window on the bottom. We do this with the split-window command. Add this line to your script:

```
tmux split-window -v -t development
```

This splits the main window in half horizontally. You could have specified a percentage using something like

```
tmux split-window -v -p 10 -t development
```

but for now, just leave the split-window command as is and then select one of the default tmux layouts—the main-horizontal one—by adding this to your script:

```
tmux select-layout -t development main-horizontal
```

We've created our first window and split it into two panes, but the bottom pane needs to open in the project folder. We already know how we send commands to tmux instances, but now we have to target those commands at specific panes and windows.

Targeting Specific Panes and Windows

With commands such as send-keys, you can specify not only the target session, but also the target window and pane. In the configuration file you created back in Chapter 2, *Configuring tmux*, on page 15, you specified a base-index of 1, meaning that your window numbering starts at 1. This base index doesn't

---

1. http://en.wikipedia.org/wiki/Carriage_return

affect the panes, though, which is why you also set the pane-base-index to 1. In our case, we have two panes in our current setup, like the following example:

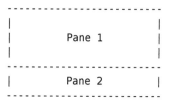

We have the Vim text editor open in Pane 1, and we want to send a command to Pane 2 that changes to our project directory. We target a pane using the format [session]:[window].[pane], so to target Pane 2, we'd use development:1.2. So, add this line to your script, and you'll get exactly what you want:

```
tmux send-keys -t development:1.2 'cd ~/devproject' C-m
```

We're almost there. Let's finish up this configuration by adding a couple more windows to the session.

Creating and Selecting Windows

We want a second window in our session that will be a full-screen console. We can create that new window using the new-window command. Add these lines to your script:

```
tmux new-window -n console -t development
tmux send-keys -t development:2 'cd ~/devproject' C-m
```

After we create the window, we use send-keys to once again change into our project directory. We only have one pane in our new window, so we only have to specify the window number in the target.

When we start up our session, we want our first window to be displayed, and we do that with the select-window command:

```
tmux select-window -t development:1
tmux attach -t development
```

We could continue to add to this script, creating additional windows and panes, starting up remote connections to our servers, tailing log files, connecting to database consoles, or even running commands that pull down the latest version of our code when we start working. But we'll stop here, and simply end our script by finally attaching to the session so it shows up on the screen, ready for us to begin working. Our entire script looks like this:

```
tmux new-session -s development -n editor -d
tmux send-keys -t development 'cd ~/devproject' C-m
tmux send-keys -t development 'vim' C-m
tmux split-window -v -t development
tmux select-layout -t development main-horizontal
tmux send-keys -t development:1.2 'cd ~/devproject' C-m
tmux new-window -n console -t development
tmux send-keys -t development:2 'cd ~/devproject' C-m
tmux select-window -t development:1
tmux attach -t development
```

When you run it with

```
$ ~/development
```

your environment will look like this:

One drawback to this approach is that this script creates a brand-new session. It won't work properly if you run it a second time while the development session is currently running. You could modify the script to check if a session with that name already exists by using the tmux has-session command and only create the session if it's not there, like this:

```
scripting/reattach/development
tmux has-session -t development
if [ $? != 0 ]
then
  tmux new-session -s development -n editor -d
  tmux send-keys -t development 'cd ~/devproject' C-m
  tmux send-keys -t development 'vim' C-m
  tmux split-window -v -t development
  tmux select-layout -t development main-horizontal
```

```
  tmux send-keys -t development:1.2 'cd ~/devproject' C-m
  tmux new-window -n console -t development
  tmux send-keys -t development:2 'cd ~/devproject' C-m
  tmux select-window -t development:1
fi
tmux attach -t development
```

This approach works well for a single project setup. You could modify this further by using a variable for the project name to make the script more generic, but let's look at a couple other ways we can configure things to manage multiple projects.

Using tmux Configuration for Setup

The .tmux.conf file itself can include commands that set up a default environment. If you wanted every tmux session to start in the same default folder, or automatically open a split window, you could bake that right in to your default configuration, simply by using the appropriate commands.

But you can also specify a configuration file when you start up an instance of tmux, by using the -f flag. This way you don't have to change your original default configuration file, and you can check your configuration file in with your project's source code. You can also set up your own per-project configuration options, such as new keyboard shortcuts to run commands or start your test suite.

Let's try this out. Create a new file called app.conf.

```
$ touch app.conf
```

Inside this file, you can use the same commands you just learned about in the previous section, but since you're inside the configuration file rather than a shell script, you don't have to explicitly prefix each command with tmux. Add this code to your app.conf file:

```
scripting/app.conf
source-file ~/.tmux.conf
new-session -s development -n editor -d
send-keys -t development 'cd ~/devproject' C-m
send-keys -t development 'vim' C-m
split-window -v -t development
select-layout -t development main-horizontal
send-keys -t development:1.2 'cd ~/devproject' C-m
new-window -n console -t development
send-keys -t development:2 'cd ~/devproject' C-m
select-window -t development:1
```

This code first loads your existing .tmux.conf file. This way you'll have all your environment settings you previously defined, including your keybindings and status bar settings. This isn't mandatory, but if you left this off, you'd have to use all the default keybindings and options, or you'd have to define your own options in this file.

To use this configuration file, pass the -f flag followed by the path to the config file. You also have to start tmux with the attach command, like this:

```
$ tmux -f app.conf attach
```

This is because, by default, tmux always calls the new-session command when it starts. This file creates a new session already, so you'd have *two* tmux sessions running if you left off attach.

This approach gives you a lot of flexibility, but you can gain even more by using a command-line tool called tmuxinator.

Managing Configuration with tmuxinator

tmuxinator is a simple tool you can use to define and manage different tmux configurations. You define window layouts and commands in a simple YAML format, and then launch them with the tmuxinator command. Unlike the other approaches, tmuxinator offers a central location for your configurations and a much easier dialect for creating complex layouts. It also lets you specify commands that should always run before each window gets created.

tmuxinator requires the Ruby interpreter, so you'll need to have that on your system. If you're on a Mac, you already have Ruby installed, and if you're on Linux, you can usually install Ruby through a package manager. However, if you plan to use Ruby for anything beyond tmuxinator, I strongly encourage you to install Ruby through RVM by following along with the instructions on the RVM website.[2]

Install tmuxinator by using Rubygems, which is the package management system for Ruby.

```
$ gem install tmuxinator
```

If you are not using RVM, you will need to run this as root or with the sudo command.

tmuxinator needs the $EDITOR shell environment to be defined, so if you haven't set yours yet, you'll want to do that in your .bashrc file on Linux, or .bash_profile

---

2.   https://rvm.io/

on macOS. For example, to define Vim as the default editor, you'd add this line to your Bash configuration:

```
export EDITOR=vim
```

Now we can create a new tmuxinator project. Let's call it "development." Execute this command:

```
$ tmuxinator open development
```

This pops open the editor you assigned to the $EDITOR environment variable and displays the default project configuration, which looks like this:

scripting/default.yaml
```
# ~/.tmuxinator/development.yml

name: development
root: ~/

# a bunch of comments....

windows:
  - editor:
      layout: main-vertical
      panes:
        - vim
        - guard
  - server: bundle exec rails s
  - logs: tail -f log/development.log
```

This is an environment that a Ruby on Rails developer who works with Git might really appreciate. This creates a tmux session with three windows. The first window is divided into two panes, using the main-vertical layout scheme. The left pane opens Vim, and the right pane opens Guard, a Ruby program that watches files for changes and executes tasks, like test runners. The second window launches Rails' built-in web server, and the third window uses the tail command to follow the application's development log file.

As you can see, tmuxinator makes it trivial to define not only the windows and panes, but also what commands we want to execute in each one. Let's use Tmuxinator to construct our development environment, with Vim in the top pane and a terminal on the bottom, starting in the ~/devproject folder. Remove the contents of this file and replace it with the following code:

scripting/development.yaml
```
name: development
root: ~/devproject
windows:
  - editor:
      layout: main-horizontal
      panes:
```

```
      - vim
      - #empty, will just run plain bash
  - console: # empty
```

The yml file format uses two spaces for indenting, so it's really important to ensure you format the file correctly and that you don't accidentally use tabs when you write the file.

To fire up the new environment, save the config file and then execute the following command:

```
$ tmuxinator development
```

tmuxinator automatically loads up your original .tmux.conf file, applies the settings, and then arranges the windows and panes for you, just like you specified. If you want to make more changes to your environment, just use

```
$ tmuxinator open development
```

again and edit the configuration.

By default, the configuration files for tmuxinator are located in ~/.tmuxinator/, so you can find those and back them up, or share them with others.

Under the hood, tmuxinator is just constructing a script that executes the individual tmux commands just like we did when we wrote our own script. However, it's a nicer syntax that's pretty easy to follow. It does require a Ruby interpreter on your machine, though, so it may not be something you'll set up on every environment where you'd like to use tmux. However, you can use Tmuxinator to generate a configuration you can use anywhere. The tmuxinator debug command can display the script that Tmuxinator will use:

```
$ tmuxinator debug development
```

Here's what the output looks like:

```
#!/bin/bash

# Clear rbenv variables before starting tmux
unset RBENV_VERSION
unset RBENV_DIR

tmux start-server;

  cd /home/brianhogan/devproject

  # Run pre command.

  # Create the session and the first window. Manually switch to root
  # directory if required to support tmux < 1.9
  TMUX= tmux new-session -d -s development -n editor
  tmux send-keys -t development:1 cd\ /home/brianhogan/devproject C-m
```

```
# Create other windows.
tmux new-window  -t development:2 -n console

# Window "editor"
tmux send-keys -t development:1.1 vim C-m

tmux splitw -c /home/brianhogan/devproject -t development:1
tmux select-layout -t development:1 tiled

tmux select-layout -t development:1 tiled

tmux select-layout -t development:1 main-horizontal
tmux select-pane -t development:1.1

# Window "console"

tmux select-window -t 1

if [ -z "$TMUX" ]; then
  tmux -u attach-session -t development
else
  tmux -u switch-client -t development
fi
```

You could save the output of tmuxinator debug to a script you can run on any machine. You can also use this option to troubleshoot any issues you might be having as you develop your configuration file.

What's Next?

You can use every tmux command through the shell, which means you can write scripts to automate nearly every aspect of tmux, including running sessions. For example, you could create a keyboard binding that sources a shell script that divides the current window into two panes and logs you into your production web and database servers.

We've covered a lot so far. You know how to set up projects, move around panes and windows, and launch your consoles. You've tinkered around with your configuration enough to understand how to customize things to your liking. And you've experimented with three separate ways to script out your tmux environment. But as you start to integrate tmux into your workflow, you'll start to notice some new issues crop up. For example, the results of tests or application logs start to scroll off the screen, and you'll want to be able to scroll up to read things. And you'll probably want to copy and paste text between panes, windows, or other applications. So let's learn how to work with tmux's output buffers next.

For Future Reference

Scriptable tmux commands

Command	Description
tmux new-session -s development -n editor	Creates a session named "development" and names the first window "editor."
tmux attach -t development	Attaches to a session named "development."
tmux send-keys -t development '[keys]' C-m	Sends the keystrokes to the "development" session's active window or pane. C-m is equivalent to pressing the Enter key.
tmux send-keys -t development:1.1 '[keys]' C-m	Sends the keystrokes to the "development" session's first window and first pane, provided the window and pane indexes are set to 1. C-m is equivalent to pressing the Enter key.
tmux select-window -t development:1	Selects the first window of "development," making it the active window.
tmux split-window -v -p 10 -t development	Splits the current window in the "development" session vertically, dividing it in half *horizontally*, and sets its height to 10% of the total window size.
tmux select-layout -t development main-horizontal	Sets the layout for the "development" session to main-horizontal.
tmux source-file [file]	Loads the specified tmux configuration file.
tmux -f app.conf attach	Loads the app.conf configuration file and attaches to a session created within the app.conf file.

tmuxinator commands

Command	Description
tmuxinator open [name]	Opens the configuration file for the project name in the default text editor. Creates the configuration if it doesn't exist.
tmuxinator [name]	Loads the tmux session for the given project. Creates the session from the contents of the project's configuration file if no session currently exists, or attaches to the session.
tmuxinator list	Lists all current projects.

Command	Description
tmuxinator copy [source] [destination]	Copies a project configuration.
tmuxinator delete [name]	Deletes the specified project.
tmuxinator implode	Deletes all current projects.
tmuxinator doctor	Looks for problems with the tmuxinator and system configuration.
tmuxinator debug	Shows the script that tmuxinator will run, helping you figure out what's going wrong.

## CHAPTER 4

Working With Text and Buffers

Throughout the course of your average day, you'll copy and paste text more times than you can keep track of. When you're working with tmux, you will eventually come to the point where you need to scroll backwards through the terminal's output buffer to see something that scrolled off the screen. You might also need to copy some text and paste it into a file or into another program. This chapter is all about how to manage the text inside your sessions. You'll see how to use the keyboard to scroll through tmux's output buffer, how to work with multiple paste buffers, and how to work with the system clipboard.

Scrolling Through Output with Copy Mode

When you work with programs in the terminal, it's common that the output from these programs scrolls off the screen. But when you use tmux, you can use the keyboard to move backwards through the output buffer so you can see what you missed. This is especially useful for those times when you're running tests or watching log files and you can't just rely on the less command or your text editor.

Pressing `Prefix` `[` places you in Copy mode. You can then use your movement keys to move the cursor around the screen. By default, the arrow keys work. But in Chapter 2, *Configuring tmux*, on page 15, you configured tmux to use Vim keys for moving between windows and resizing panes so you wouldn't have to take your hands off the home row. tmux has a vi mode for working with the buffer as well. To enable it, add this line to .tmux.conf:

buffers/tmux.conf
```
# enable vi keys.
setw -g mode-keys vi
```

With this option set, you can use `h`, `j`, `k`, and `l` to move around your buffer.

To get out of Copy mode, press the `Enter` key. Moving around one character at a time isn't very efficient. Since you enabled vi mode, you can also use some other visible shortcuts to move around the buffer.

For example, you can use `w` to jump to the next word and `b` to jump back one word. And you can use `f`, followed by any character, to jump to that character on the same line, and `F` to jump backwards on the line.

Moving Quickly Through the Buffer

When you have several pages of buffered output, moving the cursor around to scroll isn't going to be that useful. Instead of moving word by word or character by character, you can scroll through the buffer page by page, or jump to the beginning or end of the buffer.

You can move up one page with `Ctrl-b` and down one page with `Ctrl-f`. You can jump all the way to the top of the buffer's history with `g`, and then jump all the way to the bottom with `G`.

Searching Through the Buffer

You don't have to browse through the hundreds of lines of content page by page if you know what you're looking for. By pressing `?` in Copy mode, you can search upwards for phrases or keywords. Simply press `?`, type in the search phrase, and press `Enter` to jump to the first occurrence of the phrase. Then press `n` to jump to the next occurrence, or `N` to move to the previous.

To search downward, press `/` instead of `?`. Pressing `n` then jumps to the next occurrence, and `N` jumps to the previous occurrence.

Learning to move around the buffer this way will dramatically speed you up. It's faster to type the word you want to move to instead of using the arrows to move around, especially if you're looking through the output of log files.

Now let's explore how to copy text from one pane and paste it to another. This is Copy mode, after all.

Copying and Pasting Text

Moving around and looking for things in the output buffer is usually only half the equation. We often need to copy some text so we can do something useful with it. tmux's Copy mode gives us the opportunity to select and copy text to a paste buffer so we can dump that text elsewhere.

To copy text, enter Copy mode and move the cursor to where you want to start selecting text. Then press `Space` and move the cursor to the end of the text. When you press `Enter`, the selected text gets copied into a paste buffer.

To paste the contents you just captured, press `Prefix` `]`.

Let's look at a few ways to copy and paste text from our main output buffer.

Capturing a Pane

tmux has a handy shortcut that copies the entire visible contents of a pane to a paste buffer. Enter tmux's Command mode with `Prefix` `:` and type

```
capture-pane
```

The contents of the pane will be in a paste buffer. You can then paste that content into another pane or window by pressing `Prefix` `]`.

Showing and Saving the Buffer

You can display the contents of your paste buffer by using the `show-buffer` command in Command mode, or from a terminal session with

```
$ tmux show-buffer
```

However, by using the `save-buffer` command, you can save the buffer to a file, which can often be a real time saver. In fact, you can capture the contents of the current pane to a text file.

In Command mode, execute the command `capture-pane; save-buffer buffer.txt`. You could easily map that command to a keystroke if you wanted.

Using Multiple Paste Buffers

tmux maintains a stack of paste buffers, which means you can copy text without replacing the buffer's existing content. This is much more flexible than the traditional clipboard offered by the operating system.

Every time you copy some new text, tmux creates a new paste buffer, putting the new buffer at the top of the stack. To demonstrate, fire up a new tmux session and load up a text editor such as Vim or Nano. In the editor, type the following sentences, one per line:

```
First sentence is first.
Next sentence is next.
Last sentence is last.
```

Now copy some text to the paste buffer using tmux. Enter Copy mode with Prefix [. Move to the start of the first sentence, press Space to start selecting text, move to the end of the first sentence, and press Enter to copy the selection. Repeat this with the second and third sentences.

Each time you copied text, tmux created a new buffer. You can see these buffers with the list-buffers command.

```
0: 22 bytes: "Last sentence is last."
1: 22 bytes: "Next sentence is next."
2: 24 bytes: "First sentence is first."
```

Pressing Prefix] always pastes buffer 0, but you can issue the command choose-buffer to select a buffer and paste the contents into the focused pane.

Split the current window in half and launch Nano in the second pane, then enter Command mode and type this:

choose-buffer

You'll be presented with a list that looks like this:

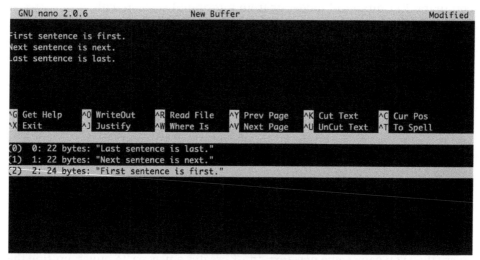

You can select any entry in the list, press Enter, and the text will be inserted into the selected pane.

This is an excellent way to manage multiple bits of text, especially in text-based environments where you don't have access to an OS-level clipboard.

These buffers are shared across *all* running tmux sessions, too, so you can take content from one session and paste it into another.

Remapping Copy and Paste Keys

If you use Vim and you'd like to make the copy and paste command keys a little more familiar, you can remap the keys in your configuration. For example, you can use `Prefix` `Escape` to enter Copy mode, then use `v` to start Visual mode to select your text, use `y` to "yank" text into the buffer, and use `p` to paste the text:

buffers/tmux.conf
```
bind Escape copy-mode
bind-key -T copy-mode-vi v send -X begin-selection
bind-key -T copy-mode-vi y send -X copy-selection
unbind p
bind p paste-buffer
```

This can be a real productivity boost if you happen to do a lot of copying and pasting between windows and panes and are already comfortable with the keys that Vim uses.

Working with the Clipboard on Linux

Using the xclip utility,[1] you can integrate your buffers with the Linux system clipboard so you can more easily copy and paste between programs.

First, you have to install xclip. On Ubuntu, use this command:

```
$ sudo apt-get install xclip
```

Then add some new keybindings to use tmux's save-buffer and set-buffer commands with xclip.

To copy the current buffer to the system clipboard, add this command to the .tmux.conf file:

buffers/linux/tmux.conf
```
# Prefix Ctrl-C takes what's in the buffer and sends it to system clipboard
# via xclip
bind C-c run "tmux save-buffer - | xclip -sel clip -i"
```

This configures `Prefix` `Ctrl`-`c` so it pipes the current buffer to xclip.

So, you enter Copy mode, select your text, press `y`, and then press `Prefix` `Ctrl`-`c` to get your text on the clipboard. You can speed up the process by binding the `y` key to send the output to xclip directly:

buffers/linux/tmux.conf
```
# y in copy mode takes selection and sends it to system clipboard via xclip
```

---

1. http://sourceforge.net/projects/xclip/

```
bind-key -T copy-mode-vi y send-keys -X copy-pipe-and-cancel "xclip -sel clip -i"
```

Now text you select and copy in Copy mode will be on your system clipboard.

To paste text from the system clipboard into a tmux session, add this line to your configuration:

buffers/linux/tmux.conf
```
# Prefix Ctrl-v fills tmux buffer from system clipboard via xclip, then
# pastes from buffer into tmux window
bind C-v run "tmux set-buffer \"$(xclip -sel clip -o)\"; tmux paste-buffer"
```

This configures tmux to pull the content from xclip into a new tmux buffer and then pastes it into the selected tmux window or pane when you press `Prefix` `Ctrl-v`.

Using macOS Clipboard Commands

If you're a Mac user, you may be familiar with macOS's command-line clipboard utilities pbcopy and pbpaste. These simple utilities make it a snap to work with the clipboard. The pbcopy command captures text to the system clipboard, and the pbpaste command pastes content out. For example, you can use pbcopy and cat together to easily put the contents of your .tmux.conf file into the clipboard so you can paste it in an email or on the web, like this:

```
$ cat ~/.tmux.conf | pbcopy
```

You can use pbcopy inside of tmux as well. For example, you can send the contents of the current tmux buffer to the system clipboard:

```
$ tmux show-buffer | pbcopy
```

Or you can paste the clipboard contents into tmux:

```
$ tmux set-buffer $(pbpaste); tmux paste-buffer
```

This means that you can also create keyboard shortcuts to do this, just like you did in *Working with the Clipboard on Linux*, on page 51.

buffers/mac/tmux.conf
```
# Prefix Ctrl-C takes what's in the buffer and sends it to system clipboard
# via pbcopy
bind C-c run "tmux save-buffer - | pbcopy"
```

To use this, first select some text and copy it to tmux's buffer. Then press `Prefix` `Ctrl-c` to copy it to the system clipboard.

That's a lot of steps. Just like with Linux, you can configure tmux's Copy mode to send the text you copy directly to the system clipboard by adding this keybinding to your configuration:

buffers/mac/tmux.conf
```
# y in copy mode takes selection and sends it to system clipboard via pbcopy
bind-key -T copy-mode-vi y send-keys -X copy-pipe-and-cancel "pbcopy"
```

Now when you select text in Copy mode and press y, the text will be sent to pbcopy and will be on your system clipboard, ready for use in other programs.

To support pasting from the system clipboard, add this longer command, which fills the buffer with the system clipboard contents and then pastes the buffer into the tmux window:

buffers/mac/tmux.conf
```
# Prefix Ctrl-v fills tmux buffer from system clipboard via pbpaste, then
# pastes from buffer into tmux window
bind C-v run "tmux set-buffer \"$(pbpaste)\"; tmux paste-buffer"
```

This provides a simple solution to an otherwise fairly complex problem.

What's Next?

By using tmux paste buffers to move text around, you gain the ability to have a clipboard in situations where you might not have one, such as when you're logged into the console of a server or without a graphical terminal. Being able to scroll back through the history of a long console output can be a huge help. It's worth installing tmux directly on your servers for that reason alone.

Now that you have a good understanding of how to find, copy, and paste text, you can start working tmux into your daily routine. For many developers, pair programming is often part of that routine. Let's take a look at how to use tmux to work with another developer.

For Future Reference

Shortcut keys

Shortcut	Description
Prefix [	Enters Copy mode.
Prefix]	Pastes current buffer contents.
Prefix =	Lists all paste buffers and pastes selected buffer contents.

Copy mode movement keys (vi mode)

Command	Description
h, j, k, and l	Moves the cursor left, down, up, and right, respectively.

Command	Description
w	Moves the cursor forward one word at a time.
b	Moves the cursor backward one word at a time.
f followed by any character	Moves to the next occurrence of the specified character.
F followed by any character	Moves to the previous occurrence of the specified character.
Ctrl-b	Scrolls up one page.
Ctrl-f	Scrolls down one page.
g	Jumps to the top of the buffer.
G	Jumps to the bottom of the buffer.
?	Starts a search backward through the buffer.
/	Starts a search forward through the buffer.

Commands

Command	Description
show-buffer	Displays current buffer contents.
capture-pane	Captures the selected pane's visible contents to a new buffer.
list-buffers	Lists all paste buffers.
choose-buffer	Shows paste buffers and pastes the contents of the one you select.
save-buffer [filename]	Saves the buffer's contents to the specified file.

## CHAPTER 5

Pair Programming with tmux

Up until now, you've been making configuration changes and learning how to work within tmux on your own machine. But one of the most popular uses of tmux by developers is pair programming. It was actually my first introduction to tmux, and I immediately saw the potential as my friend walked me through using its various features.

Pair programming has a lot of great benefits. Working with another developer can help you see things you might not have seen on your own, but unless you're physically in the same location, pair programming can be somewhat difficult. Screen-sharing through iChat, Skype, or even GoToMeeting takes up a lot of bandwidth and can be dodgy when you're not using the best network connection. In this chapter, we'll explore using tmux for pair programming, so you can work remotely with another developer on even the slowest hotel Wi-Fi connection.

There are two ways to work with remote users. The first method involves creating a new user account that you and others share. You set up tmux and your development environment under that account and use it as a shared workspace. The second approach uses tmux's sockets so you can have a second user connect to your tmux session without having to share your user account.

Both of these methods have an inherent security flaw: they let someone else see things on your screen and in your account. You're inviting someone in to potentially look at your files. To get around this, it's wise to use an intermediate server for pairing. Using a low-cost VPS or a virtual machine with VirtualBox[1] and Vagrant[2], you can quickly create a development environment

---

1. https://www.virtualbox.org/
2. https://www.vagrantup.com/docs/getting-started/

for pairing. In this chapter, we'll be working with a remote server as we explore both of these approaches.

Pairing with a Shared Account

Using a shared account is the simplest way to work with another user. In a nutshell, you enable SSH access on the machine that will act as the host, install and configure tmux on that machine, and then create a tmux session there. The second user logs into that machine with the same user account and attaches to the session. By using SSH public keys, you can make the login process somewhat transparent. Let's walk through the setup. For this example, we'll use a server called puzzles running Ubuntu that has the SSH daemon installed.

First, create a "tmux" user on the server. This is the user everyone will use to connect to the pairing session. On the remote server, execute this command:

```
tmux@puzzles$ adduser tmux
```

We want to configure the account so we can take SSH keys from other developers and use them to log into this account. We do this by creating the file ~/.ssh/authorized_keys under the tmux account. So, use the su command to switch to the user:

```
tmux@puzzles$ su tmux
```

Then create the .ssh folder and the .ssh/authorized_keys file, setting the appropriate permissions. Only the tmux user should be allowed to read, write, or execute the folder and file.

```
tmux@puzzles$ mkdir ~/.ssh
tmux@puzzles$ touch ~/.ssh/authorized_keys
tmux@puzzles$ chmod 700 ~/.ssh
tmux@puzzles$ chmod 600 ~/.ssh/authorized_keys
```

Each user you'd like to connect needs a public key, which they would generate on their local machine. To generate a key, use the command

```
$ ssh-keygen
```

and follow the prompts on the screen.

Then each user would transfer their public key over to the server and add it to the authorized_keys file. There are a number of ways to do this, but the most universal approach would be to use cat and ssh to transfer the key and append it to authorized_keys at the same time, like this:

```
$ cat ~/.ssh/id_rsa.pub | ssh tmux@your_server 'cat >> .ssh/authorized_keys'
```

You'll be prompted for the tmux user's password before you can connect.

The command ssh-copy-id makes this process slightly easier. If you install this command using your package manager on your client, then you can transfer the key like this:

```
$ ssh-copy-id tmux@your_server
```

This copies the .id_rsa.pub file automatically.

You would repeat this process for any other users you wanted to share this account with.

Then on the remote server, you'd set up tmux, text editors, compilers, programming languages, and version control systems just like you would on any other development environment. Then you create a new tmux session on the server:

```
tmux@puzzles$ tmux new-session -s Pairing
```

Another member of your team can log in to the same machine and attach to the session with this:

```
tmux@puzzles$ tmux attach -t Pairing
```

You can then work collaboratively on the project. What's more, you can detach from the session and reattach to it later, which means you can leave your environment running for days or even weeks at a time. You'd have a persistent development environment you can log into from anywhere that has a terminal with SSH support.

Using a Shared Account and Grouped Sessions

When two people are attached to the same tmux session, they usually both see the same thing and interact with the same windows. But there are times when it's helpful if one person can work in a different window without completely taking over control.

Using "grouped sessions," you can do just that. Let's demonstrate by creating a new session on our remote server called groupedsession.

```
tmux@puzzles$ tmux new-session -s groupedsession
```

Then, instead of attaching to the session, another user can join that session by *creating a new session* by specifying the target of the original session groupedsession and then specifying their *own* session name, like this:

```
tmux@puzzles$ tmux new-session -t groupedsession -s mysession
```

When the second session launches, both users can interact with the session at the same time, just as if the second user had attached to the session. However, the users can create windows independent of each other. So, if our new user creates a window, you'll both see the new window show up in the status line, but you'll stay on the window you're currently working in! This is great for those "Hey, let me just try something" moments, or when one person wants to use Emacs and the other person prefers Vim:

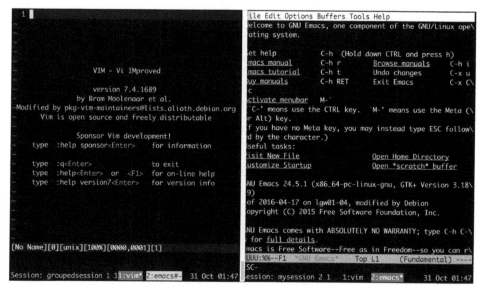

The second user can kill off their session with kill-session, and the original will still exist. However, both sessions will be killed if all windows are closed, so be careful!

That's a lot of work to go through if you just want someone to jump in and help you out with some code. So let's look at a simple alternative that takes almost no time to set up.

Quickly Pairing with tmate

tmate[3] is a fork of tmux designed to make pair programming painless. Using tmate, you can quickly invite another developer to collaborate. When you launch tmate, it generates an address that your pair can use to make the connection. You don't have to set up any keys or use any intermediate services. Instead, tmate's servers handle tunneling the connection for you.

---

3.   https://tmate.io/

The catch is that you have to install tmate and use it instead of tmux. But don't worry; it completely supports the configuration you've already built. Let's look at how to get it installed.

On Ubuntu, you can install it by adding the tmate PPA to your package manager:

```
$ sudo apt-get install software-properties-common
$ sudo add-apt-repository ppa:tmate.io/archive
$ sudo apt-get update && sudo apt-get install tmate
```

On the Mac, you can install it with Homebrew:

```
$ brew install tmate
```

Once tmate is installed, fire it up with

```
$ tmate
```

and tmate will launch, displaying the connection address in the bottom of the window where your status line would be.

Copy that address and send it to your pair, and they'll be able to join you instantly. If the address disappears before you can copy it, or you'd like to see it again, execute the command

```
$ tmate show-messages
```

to view the address again, along with some other interesting details, including a read-only address you can send to someone if you just want to demonstrate something and don't want them to have any control:

```
Sun Sep 25 17:46:13 2016 [tmate] Connecting to ssh.tmate.io...
Sun Sep 25 17:46:13 2016 [tmate] Note: clear your terminal before sharing readonly
access
Sun Sep 25 17:46:13 2016 [tmate] web session read only: https://...
Sun Sep 25 17:46:13 2016 [tmate] ssh session read only: ssh ...
Sun Sep 25 17:46:13 2016 [tmate] web session: https://...
Sun Sep 25 17:46:13 2016 [tmate] ssh session: ssh ...
```

tmate supports the same commands that tmux supports, so you can create named sessions and even script up your configurations. You can even use it with Tmuxinator by adding the following to your Tmuxinator YAML file:

```
tmux_options: -S /tmp/your_project_name_tmate_socket
tmux_command: tmate
```

Since tmate creates a randomly named socket file, we just tell it not to do that by passing the -S switch. Then we tell Tmuxinator that it should use tmate instead of tmux.

Using tmate with Your Own Servers

If you feel uncomfortable going through ssh.tmate.io to connect to other sessions, you can find instructions for setting up your own server at the tmate website.[a] It provides you with the server, which you compile and install on your own Linux server. Then you run the server and configure client machines to use that server instead of the default service. This may add more security, but you'll want to think about redundancy and availability. For example, the tmate.io address resolves to multiple backend servers, ensuring high availability. If you want to ensure continuity, you'll want to configure your environment in a similar way.

---

a.   https://tmate.io/

Using shared accounts or tmate is easy, but it's not always desirable to share user accounts with team members or let someone remotely access your development machine. Let's look at an alternative approach.

Pairing with Separate Accounts and Sockets

Using tmux's support for sockets, you can create sessions that multiple users can connect to with ease.

To test this out, create two new user accounts for the session: one called "ted" and another named "barney."

```
tmux@puzzles$ sudo adduser ted
```

```
tmux@puzzles$ sudo adduser barney
```

Next, create the "tmux" group and the /var/tmux folder that will hold the shared sessions.

```
tmux@puzzles$ sudo addgroup tmux
```

```
tmux@puzzles$ sudo mkdir /var/tmux
```

Next, change the group ownership of the /var/tmux folder so that the tmux group has access:

```
tmux@puzzles$ sudo chgrp tmux /var/tmux
```

Then alter the permissions on the folder so that new files will be accessible for all members of the tmux group:

```
tmux@puzzles$ sudo chmod g+ws /var/tmux
```

Finally, add ted and barney to the tmux group.

```
tmux@puzzles$ sudo usermod -aG tmux ted
```

```
tmux@puzzles$ sudo usermod -aG tmux barney
```

Now let's look at how these users can work together on a project.

Creating and Sharing Sessions

So far, you've used the new-session command to create these sessions, but that uses the default socket location, which won't be reachable by every user. Instead of creating named sessions, we create our sessions using the -S switch.

Log in to your server as ted and create a new tmux session using a socket file in the /var/tmux/ folder:

```
ted@puzzles$ tmux -S /var/tmux/pairing
```

In another terminal window, log in as barney and then attach to the session. But instead of specifying the target with the -t switch, specify the location of the socket file, like this:

```
barney@puzzles$ tmux -S /var/tmux/pairing attach
```

The barney user now attaches to the tmux session and sees everything that the ted user sees.

It's important to note that when using this approach, the .tmux.conf file used is the one that started up the session. Having two separate accounts doesn't mean that each account gets to use its own configuration files within the tmux session, but it does mean they can customize their accounts for other purposes, and can each initiate their own tmux session as needed. More importantly, it keeps barney out of ted's home directory.

What's Next?

Now that you know how to use tmux to share your screen with others, you can use it for remote training, impromptu collaboration on open source projects, or even presentations.

In addition, you could use this technique to fire up a tmux session on one of your production servers, load up monitoring tools or consoles, and then detach from it, leaving those tools running in the background. Then you simply connect to your machine, reattach to the session, and everything is back where you left it. I do something similar with my development environment. I set up tmux on a VPS, which lets me use nothing more than an iPad, an SSH client, and a Bluetooth keyboard to hack on code when I'm away from home. It even works brilliantly over the 3G network.

Pair programming and working remotely are just two examples of how incorporating tmux into your workflow can make you more productive. In the next chapter, we'll look at other enhancements we can make to our environment as we explore advanced ways to work with windows, panes, and our system in general.

For Future Reference

Command	Description
tmux new-session -t [existing session] -s [new session]	Creates a connection to a grouped session.
tmux show-messages	Displays a log of messages in the current window, useful for debugging.
tmux -S [socket]	Creates a new session using a socket instead of a name.
tmux -S [socket] attach	Attaches to an existing session using a socket instead of a name.

## CHAPTER 6

Workflows

By itself, tmux is just another terminal with a few bells and whistles that let us display...more terminal sessions. But tmux makes it easier to work with the programs we run in those sessions, so this chapter will explore some common, and uncommon, configurations and commands that you may find useful in your day-to-day work. You'll see some advanced ways to manage your panes and sessions, how to make tmux work with your shell of choice, how to extend tmux commands with external scripts, and how to create key-bindings that execute several commands. Let's start with windows and panes.

Working Effectively with Panes and Windows

Throughout this book, you've seen ways to divide up your tmux sessions into panes and windows. In this section, we'll look at more advanced ways to work with those panes and windows.

Turning a Pane into a Window

Panes are great for dividing up a workspace, but sometimes you might want to "pop out" a pane into its own window. tmux has a command to do just that.

Inside any pane, press `Prefix !` and tmux will create a new window from your pane, removing the original pane.

Turning a Window into a Pane

Occasionally, it's nice to consolidate a workspace. You can easily take a window and turn it into a pane. To do this, issue the join-pane command.

Try it out. Create a new tmux session with two windows.

```
$ tmux new-session -s panes -n first -d
$ tmux new-window -t panes -n second
$ tmux attach -t panes
```

Now, to move the first window into a pane in the second window, press `Prefix` `:` to enter Command mode, and type this:

join-pane -s panes:1

This means "Take window 1 of the panes session and join it to the current window," since we did not specify a target. When you "join" a pane, you're essentially moving a pane from one session to another. You specify the source window and pane, followed by the target window and pane. If you leave the target off, the current focused window becomes the target.

You can use this technique to move panes around as well. If your first window had two panes, you could specify the source pane like this, keeping in mind that you set the window and pane base indexes to 1 instead of 0 back in Chapter 2, *Configuring tmux*, on page 15.

join-pane -s panes:1.1

This command grabs the first pane of the first window and joins it to the current window.

To take it a step further, you can specify a different source session, using the notation [session_name]:[window].[pane], and you can specify a target window using the -t flag using the same notation. This lets you pull panes from one session into another.

Maximizing and Restoring Panes

Sometimes you just want a pane to go full-screen for a bit so you can see its contents or work in a more focused way. You could use the break-pane command. But then you'd have to use join-pane to put it back where it was. But there's a better way. The resize-pane command accepts the -Z option for zooming a pane. Best of all, it's already mapped to `Prefix` `z`, and pressing it again restores the pane to its original size.

Launching Commands in Panes

In Chapter 3, *Scripting Customized tmux Environments*, on page 35, we explored how to use shell commands and send-keys to launch programs in our panes, but we can execute commands automatically when we launch a window or a pane.

We have two servers, burns and smithers, which run our web server and database server, respectively. When we start up tmux, we want to connect to these servers using a single window with two panes.

Let's create a new script called servers.sh and create one session connecting to two servers:

```
$ tmux new-session -s servers -d "ssh deploy@burns"
$ tmux split-window -v "ssh dba@smithers"
$ tmux attach -t servers
```

When we create a new session, we can pass the command we want to execute as the last argument. In our case, we fire off the new session and connect to burns in the first window, and we detach the session. Then we divide the window using a vertical split and then connect to smithers.

This configuration has a handy side effect: when we log off of our remote servers, the pane or window will close.

Opening a Pane in the Current Directory

When you open a new pane, tmux places you in the directory where you originally launched tmux. Sometimes that's exactly what you want, but if you navigated into another directory, you might want to create a new pane that starts in that directory instead.

You can use the pane_current_path variable provided by tmux when creating a new pane. Open Command mode and execute

```
split-window -v -c  "#{pane_current_path}"
```

This splits the window horizontally, but opens the new terminal session in the same working directory as the current pane or window.

You can add this to your configuration file to make this easy. Instead of changing the existing bindings for splits, add new ones so you can choose the behavior you'd like:

workflows/tmux.conf
```
# split pane and retain the current directory of existing pane
bind _ split-window -v -c  "#{pane_current_path}"
bind \ split-window -h -c "#{pane_current_path}"
```

This configures things so that `Prefix` `_` splits the window horizontally and `Prefix` `/` splits the window vertically.

Issuing Commands in Many Panes Simultaneously

Every once in a while, you might need to execute the same command in multiple panes. You might need to run the same update script on two servers, for example. You can do this easily with tmux.

Using the command set-window-option synchronize-panes on, anything you type in one pane will be immediately broadcast to the other panes in the current session. Once you've issued the command, you can turn it off with set-window-option synchronize-panes off.

To make this easier to do, you can map this to Prefix Ctrl-s, like this:

workflows/tmux.conf
```
# shortcut for synchronize-panes toggle
bind C-s set-window-option synchronize-panes
```

By not specifying the off or on option, the synchronize-panes command acts as a toggle. While this isn't something you'll use very often, it's amazingly handy when you need it.

Managing Sessions

As you get more comfortable with tmux, you may find yourself using more than one tmux session simultaneously. For example, you may fire up unique tmux sessions for each application you're working on so you can keep the environments contained. There are some great tmux features to make managing these sessions painless.

Moving Between Sessions

All tmux sessions on a single machine route through a single server. That means you can move effortlessly between your sessions from a single client.

Let's try this out. Start two detached tmux sessions, one named "editor," which launches Vim, and the other running the top command, called "processes":

```
$ tmux new -s editor -d vim
$ tmux new -s processes -d top
```

Connect to the "editor" session with

```
$ tmux attach -t editor
```

and then press Prefix (to go to the previous session and Prefix) to move to the next session.

You can also use Prefix s to display a list of sessions, so you can quickly navigate between sessions:

```
(0) + editor: 1 windows (attached)
(1) + processes: 1 windows
```

You can use the j and k keys to move up and down if you've configured tmux to use Vim-like movement, and you can press Space to expand a session so you can jump to a specific window or pane.

You can add custom keybindings for this to your .tmux.conf file by binding keys to the switch-client command. The default configuration looks like this:

```
bind  ( switch-client -p
bind  ) switch-client -n
```

If you've set up multiple workspaces, this is an extremely efficient way to move around your environments, without detaching and reattaching.

Moving Windows Between Sessions

You can move a window from one session to another. This is handy in case you've started up a process in one environment and want to move it around or want to consolidate your workspaces.

The move-window command is mapped to Prefix . (the period), so you can bring up the window you want to move, press the key combination, and then type the name of the target session.

To try this out, create two sessions, with the names "editor" and "processes," running vim and top respectively:

```
$ tmux new -s editor -d vim
$ tmux new -s processes -d top
```

Let's move the window in the "processes" session into the "editor" session.

First, attach to the "processes" session with this:

```
$ tmux attach -t processes
```

Then, press Prefix . and type "editor" in the command line that appears.

This removes the only window in the "processes" session, causing it to close. If you attach to the "editor" session, you'll see both windows.

You can use shell commands to do this, too, so you don't need to consolidate things by opening sessions. To do that, use move-window, like this:

```
$ tmux move-window -s processes:1 -t editor
```

This moves the first window of the "processes" session to the "editor" session.

Creating or Attaching to Existing Sessions

So far, we've always taken the approach of creating new tmux sessions whenever we want to work. However, we can actually detect if a tmux session exists and connect to it if it does.

The has-session command returns a Boolean value that we can use in a shell script. That means we can do something like this in a Bash script:

```
if ! tmux has-session -t development; then
  exec tmux new-session -s development -d
  # other setup commands before attaching....
fi
exec tmux attach -t development
```

If you modify the script to take an argument, you can use this to create a single script that you can use to connect to or create any tmux session.

tmux and Your Operating System

As tmux becomes part of your workflow, you may want to integrate it more tightly with your operating system. In this section, you'll discover ways to make tmux and your system work well together.

Using a Different Shell

In this book, we've used the Bash shell, but if you're a fan of zsh, you can still get all the tmux goodness.

Just explicitly set the default shell in .tmux.conf like this:

```
set -g default-shell /bin/zsh
```

Since tmux is just a terminal multiplexer and not a shell of its own, you just specify exactly what to run when it starts.

Launching tmux by Default

You can configure your system to launch tmux automatically when you open a terminal. And using what you know about session names, you can create a new session if one doesn't exist, or attach to one that does.

When tmux is running, it sets the TERM variable to "screen" or the value of the default-terminal setting in the configuration file. You can use this value in your .bashrc (or .bash_profile on macOS) file to determine whether or not you're currently in a tmux session. You set your tmux terminal to "screen-256color" back in Chapter 2, *Configuring tmux*, on page 15, so you could use that to detect if tmux is actually running.

For example, you could add these lines to the end of your .bashrc file:

```
if [[ -z "$TMUX" ]]; then
  tmux new-session -A -s "$USER"
fi
```

This first checks that you're not already in a tmux session by looking for an environment variable called TMUX, which will exist if you're in a TMUX session. If you're not already in a session, it then creates or attaches to a session with a session name of $USER, which is your username. You can replace this with any value you want, but using the username helps avoid conflicts.

When the tmux session starts up, it will run through your .bashrc or .bash_profile file again, but this time it will see that you're in a tmux session, skip over this chunk of code, and execute the rest of the commands in your configuration file, ensuring that all your environment variables are set for you.

Now every time you open a new terminal, you'll be in a tmux session. Be careful, though, since each time you open a new terminal session on your machine, it will be attached to the same session. Exiting tmux in one terminal will exit tmux in all of them.

Keeping Specific Configuration Separate

In Chapter 4, *Working With Text and Buffers*, on page 47, you learned how to make tmux work with the macOS and Linux system clipboards, and this involved adding some specific configuration options to your .tmux.conf file. But if you wanted your configuration to work on both operating systems, you'd run into some conflicts.

The solution is to move your OS-specific configuration into a separate file and then tell tmux to load it up by using tmux's if-shell command and the source command.

Try it out. Create a new file called .tmux.mac.conf in your home directory:

```
$ touch ~/.tmux.mac.conf
```

In that file, put all the code to make the Mac's clipboard work with tmux:

workflows/tmux.mac.conf
```
# Prefix Ctrl-C takes what's in the buffer and sends it to system clipboard
# via pbcopy
bind C-c run "tmux save-buffer - | pbcopy"

# y in copy mode takes selection and sends it to system clipboard via pbcopy
bind-key -T copy-mode-vi y send-keys -X copy-pipe-and-cancel "pbcopy"

# Prefix Ctrl-v fills tmux buffer from system clipboard via pbpaste, then
```

```
# pastes from buffer into tmux window
bind C-v run "tmux set-buffer \"$(pbpaste)\"; tmux paste-buffer"
```

Then open .tmux.conf and remove any lines related to macOS if you've put them in. Then add this to the end of the file:

workflows/tmux.conf

```
# Load mac-specific settings
if-shell "uname | grep -q Darwin" "source-file ~/.tmux.mac.conf"
```

The if-shell command runs a shell command, and if it was successful, it executes the step. In this case, we tell tmux to run the uname command and use grep to see if it contains the word "Darwin." If it does, it's a safe bet we're on a Mac, so we load the configuration file.

You could use a similar approach to load an additional bit of configuration only if it exists. For example, you may want to share your main .tmux.conf file with the world on GitHub, but you may want to keep some of your own secret sauce private. So move all of those tricks into .tmux.private, and add this to your .tmux.conf file:

workflows/tmux.conf

```
# load private settings if they exist
if-shell "[ -f ~/.tmux.private]" "source ~/.tmux.private"
```

This will only load the file if it exists.

Recording Program Output to a Log

Sometimes it's useful to be able to capture the output of a terminal session to a log. You already learned how to use capture-pane and save-buffer to do this, but tmux can actually record the activity in a pane right to a text file with the pipe-pane command. This is similar to the script command available in many shells, except that with pipe-pane, you can toggle it on and off at will, and you can start it after a program is already running.

To activate this, enter Command mode and type pipe-pane -o "cat >> mylog.txt".

You can use the -o flag to toggle the output, which means if you send the exact command again, you can turn the logging off. To make it easier to execute this command, add this to your configuration script as a shortcut key.

workflows/tmux.conf

```
# Log output to a text file on demand
bind P pipe-pane -o "cat >>~/#W.log" \; display "Toggled logging to ~/#W.log"
```

Now you can press Prefix P to toggle logging. Thanks to the display command (short for display-message), you'll see the name of the log file displayed in the status line. The display command has access to the same variables as the status line, which you learned about in Table 1, *Status Line Variables*, on page 28.

Adding Battery Life to the Status Line

If you use tmux on a laptop, you may want to show the remaining battery life in your status line, especially if you run your terminal in full-screen mode. It turns out that this is a simple thing to add thanks to the #(shell-command) variable.

Let's add the battery status to our configuration file. Grab a shell script that can fetch the remaining battery charge and display it to the screen. We'll place this in a file called battery in our home folder and tell tmux to run it for us.

First, download the file:

```
$ wget --no-check-certificate \
https://raw.github.com/richo/battery/master/bin/battery
```

You can also find the battery script in the book's source code downloads.

Now make it executable so tmux can use it:

```
$ chmod +x ~/battery
```

Test it out by running

```
$ ~/battery Discharging
```

If you're running this on a laptop without the power cord plugged in, you'll see the percentage left on the battery.

We can get tmux to display the output of any command-line program in its status bar by using #(<command>). So, to display the battery in front of the clock, change the status-right line in .tmux.conf to this:

```
# Status line right side -  50% | 31 Oct 13:37
set -g status-right "#(~/battery Discharging) | #[fg=cyan]%d %b %R"
```

Now, when you reload the .tmux.conf file, the battery status indicator will appear.

```
Session: development 1 1  1:editor* 2:webserver# 3:dbconsole-    26% | 30 Jan 21:49
```

To get battery status when it's charging, you'll need to execute the command

```
$ ~/battery Charging
```

and work that into the status line. I'll leave that up to you.

You can use this approach to customize your status line further. You'd simply need to write your own script that returns the value you want to display, and then drop it into the status line.

Integrating Seamlessly with Vim

The Vim text editor works pretty well with tmux, but developer Mislav Marohnić developed a solution that lets you move between tmux panes and Vim splits seamlessly. To make this work, you'll need to install Chris Toomey's vim-tmux-navigator plugin for Vim[1] and add some keybindings to your .tmux.conf file.

This setup will create the following keybindings:

- Ctrl-j moves up
- Ctrl-k moves down
- Ctrl-h moves left
- Ctrl-l moves right

If you're in tmux and you move into Vim, then the Vim plugin will take over. If you're in Vim and you move to tmux, then tmux will take over. Instead of having to learn two sets of commands to navigate, you just have one. To set this up, install the Vim plugin using Vundle by adding this to your .vimrc file:

```
Plugin 'christoomey/vim-tmux-navigator'
```

Then save your .vimrc file and run

```
:PluginInstall
```

in Vim to install the plugin.

Then in .tmux.conf, add these lines:

workflows/tmux.conf
```
is_vim="ps -o state= -o comm= -t '#{pane_tty}' \
    | grep -iqE '^[^TXZ ]+ +(\\S+\\/)?g?(view|n?vim?x?)(diff)?$'"
bind-key -n C-h if-shell "$is_vim" "send-keys C-h"  "select-pane -L"
bind-key -n C-j if-shell "$is_vim" "send-keys C-j"  "select-pane -D"
bind-key -n C-k if-shell "$is_vim" "send-keys C-k"  "select-pane -U"
bind-key -n C-l if-shell "$is_vim" "send-keys C-l"  "select-pane -R"
bind-key -n C-\ if-shell "$is_vim" "send-keys C-\\" "select-pane -l"

bind C-l send-keys 'C-l'
```

---

1. https://github.com/christoomey/vim-tmux-navigator

Ctrl-l is the keybinding used by the readline library in many shells for clearing the screen. The last line of this configuration sets up Prefix Ctrl-l to issue that command instead.

Extending tmux with Plugins

So far, we've made modifications directly to the tmux configuration file. While that works, it can be a little awkward when doing something more complex. Bruno Sutic developed a solution to this called TPM, the tmux plugin manager. Since then, more and more people have come together to build plugins to extend tmux. Let's use TPM to install the incredibly useful tmux-resurrect[2] plugin, which can restore tmux sessions even after a reboot!

To set it up, first clone the repository into a folder called ~/.tmux/plugins/tpm:

```
$ git clone https://github.com/tmux-plugins/tpm ~/.tmux/plugins/tpm
```

Then add these lines to your .tmux.conf file:

```
workflows/tmux.conf
set -g @plugin 'tmux-plugins/tpm'
set -g @plugin 'tmux-plugins/tmux-resurrect'
run '~/.tmux/plugins/tpm/tpm'
```

First we list TPM itself, followed by the tmux-resurrect plugin. Then we load TPM so it can load other plugins. Save this file and reload your configuration. Then press Prefix I to install the plugin. You'll see this output in tmux:

```
Already installed "tpm"

Installing "tmux-resurrect"
  "tmux-resurrect" download success

TMUX environment reloaded.

Done, press ENTER to continue.
```

Now test out the tmux-resurrect program. Open a couple more panes, and then press Prefix Ctrl-s to save the state of the tmux session. Then close all of the panes and exit tmux. Finally, reload tmux and press Prefix Ctrl-r to restore the session you saved. All of your panes will come back!

Visit the list of tmux plugins[3] and find one you'd like to install. You'll find one for the battery meter we set up, another for OS-specific clipboard support, and even one with sensible configuration options similar to the ones you've

---

2. https://github.com/tmux-plugins/tmux-resurrect
3. https://github.com/tmux-plugins

configured in this book. Experiment with each of these and find a configuration that's right for you.

What's Next?

There's so much more you can do with tmux now that you know the basics and you've had some experience playing around with various configurations. The tmux manual, which you can access from your terminal with

```
$ man tmux
```

has the complete list of configuration options and available commands.

And don't forget that tmux itself is rapidly evolving. The next version will bring new configuration options, which will give you even more flexibility.

As you integrate tmux into your workflow, you may discover other techniques you start to rely on. For example, you can use tmux and a text-based editor on a remote server to create an incredibly effective development environment that you can use to collaborate with another developer. You can even use irssi (a terminal-based IRC client) and Alpine (a terminal-based email app) within your tmux sessions, either alongside of your text editor in a pane, or in background windows. Then you can detach from the session and come back to it later, with your entire environment ready to go.

Keep working with tmux and before you know it, it'll be an indispensable part of your workflow.

For Future Reference

Command	Description
Prefix !	Converts the currently selected pane into a new window.
join-pane -s [session]:[window].[pane]	Converts the specified session's window or pane into a pane in the current window.
join-pane -s [session]:[window].[pane] -t [other session]	Converts the specified session's window or pane into a pane in the target session.
Prefix z	Zooms the current pane, making it full screen. Pressing it again restores the pane to its original size.
tmux new-session "[command]"	Launches tmux and executes a command. When the command completes, the tmux session closes.

Command	Description
split-pane "[command]"	Splits the current window and executes the specified command in the new pane. When the command completes, the pane closes.
split-window -c "#{pane_current_path}"	Splits the pane and sets the working directory of the new pane to the current working directory of the focused pane.
set-window-option synchronize-panes	Toggles pane synchronization, where keystrokes are issued to all panes simultaneously instead of only the current pane.
Prefix (	Moves to the next tmux session.
Prefix)	Moves to the previous tmux session.
Prefix s	Shows the session selection list.
move-window -s [source session]: [window] -t [target session]	Moves a window from one session to another. Also available with Prefix ., followed by the target session name.
set -g default-shell [shell]	Sets the default shell that tmux uses when creating new windows.
set -g default-command [command]	Sets the default command that tmux uses when creating new windows. Blank by default.
if-shell "[condition]" "[command]"	Performs a given *command* if the *condition* evaluates to true.
pipe-pane -o "cat >>~/#W.log"	Records the current pane to a text file.

Our Configuration

Throughout the book, we've built up a somewhat complex .tmux.conf file. Here's the entire file for your reference.

workflows/tmux.conf
```
# Setting the prefix from C-b to C-a
set -g prefix C-a
#
# Free the original Ctrl-b prefix keybinding
unbind C-b
#
#setting the delay between prefix and command
set -s escape-time 1
#
# Ensure that we can send Ctrl-A to other apps
bind C-a send-prefix

# Set the base index for windows to 1 instead of 0
set -g base-index 1

# Set the base index for panes to 1 instead of 0
setw -g pane-base-index 1

# Reload the file with Prefix r
bind r source-file ~/.tmux.conf \; display "Reloaded!"

# splitting panes with | and -
bind | split-window -h
bind - split-window -v

# moving between panes with Prefix h,j,k,l
bind h select-pane -L
bind j select-pane -D
bind k select-pane -U
bind l select-pane -R
```

```
# Quick window selection
bind -r C-h select-window -t :-
bind -r C-l select-window -t :+

# Pane resizing panes with Prefix H,J,K,L
bind -r H resize-pane -L 5
bind -r J resize-pane -D 5
bind -r K resize-pane -U 5
bind -r L resize-pane -R 5

# mouse support - set to on if you want to use the mouse
set -g mouse off

# Set the default terminal mode to 256color mode
set -g default-terminal "screen-256color"

# set the status line's colors
set -g status-style fg=white,bg=black

# set the color of the window list
setw -g window-status-style fg=cyan,bg=black

# set colors for the active window
setw -g window-status-current-style fg=white,bold,bg=red

# colors for pane borders
setw -g pane-border-style fg=green,bg=black
setw -g pane-active-border-style fg=white,bg=yellow

# active pane normal, other shaded out
setw -g window-style fg=colour240,bg=colour235
setw -g window-active-style fg=white,bg=black

# Command / message line
setw -g message-style fg=white,bold,bg=black

# Status line left side to show Session:window:pane
set -g status-left-length 40
set -g status-left "#[fg=green]Session: #S #[fg=yellow]#I #[fg=cyan]#P"

# Status line right side -  50% | 31 Oct 13:37
set -g status-right "#(~/battery Discharging) | #[fg=cyan]%d %b %R"

# Update the status line every sixty seconds
set -g status-interval 60

# Center the window list in the status line
set -g status-justify centre

# enable activity alerts
setw -g monitor-activity on
set -g visual-activity on

# enable vi keys.
setw -g mode-keys vi

# escape turns on copy mode
bind Escape copy-mode-vi
```

```
# v in copy mode starts making selection
bind-key -T copy-mode-vi v send -X begin-selection

# make Prefix p paste the buffer.
unbind p
bind p paste-buffer

# shortcut for synchronize-panes toggle
bind C-s set-window-option synchronize-panes

# split pane and retain the current directory of existing pane
bind _ split-window -v -c  "#{pane_current_path}"
bind \ split-window -h -c "#{pane_current_path}"

# Log output to a text file on demand
bind P pipe-pane -o "cat >>~/#W.log" \; display "Toggled logging to ~/#W.log"
#
# Load mac-specific settings
if-shell "uname | grep -q Darwin" "source-file ~/.tmux.mac.conf"

# load private settings if they exist
if-shell "[ -f ~/.tmux.private]" "source ~/.tmux.private"

is_vim="ps -o state= -o comm= -t '#{pane_tty}' \
    | grep -iqE '^[^TXZ ]+ +(\\S+\|\/)?g?(view|n?vim?x?)(diff)?$'"
bind-key -n C-h if-shell "$is_vim" "send-keys C-h"  "select-pane -L"
bind-key -n C-j if-shell "$is_vim" "send-keys C-j"  "select-pane -D"
bind-key -n C-k if-shell "$is_vim" "send-keys C-k"  "select-pane -U"
bind-key -n C-l if-shell "$is_vim" "send-keys C-l"  "select-pane -R"
bind-key -n C-\ if-shell "$is_vim" "send-keys C-\\" "select-pane -l"

bind C-l send-keys 'C-l'

set -g @plugin 'tmux-plugins/tpm'
set -g @plugin 'tmux-plugins/tmux-resurrect'
run '~/.tmux/plugins/tpm/tpm'
```

Also by the Author

Improve your skills in HTML, CSS, and programming.

HTML5 and CSS3 (2nd edition)

HTML5 and CSS3 are more than just buzzwords –
they're the foundation for today's web applications.
This book gets you up to speed on the HTML5 elements
and CSS3 features you can use right now in your current projects, with backwards compatible solutions
that ensure that you don't leave users of older browsers
behind. This new edition covers even more new features, including CSS animations, IndexedDB, and
client-side validations.

Brian P. Hogan
(314 pages) ISBN: 9781937785598. $38
https://pragprog.com/book/bhh52e

Exercises for Programmers

When you write software, you need to be at the top of
your game. Great programmers practice to keep their
skills sharp. Get sharp and stay sharp with more than
fifty practice exercises rooted in real-world scenarios.
If you're a new programmer, these challenges will help
you learn what you need to break into the field, and if
you're a seasoned pro, you can use these exercises to
learn that hot new language for your next gig.

Brian P. Hogan
(118 pages) ISBN: 9781680501223. $24
https://pragprog.com/book/bhwb

Tools for the Web

Each new version of the web brings its own gold rush. Here are your tools.

Web Development Recipes 2nd Edition

Modern web development is so much more than just HTML and CSS with a little JavaScript mixed in. People want faster, more usable interfaces that work on multiple devices, and you need the latest tools and techniques to make that happen. This book gives you over 40 concise solutions to today's web development problems, and introduces new solutions that will expand your skill set – proven, practical advice from authors who use these tools and techniques every day. In this completely updated edition, you'll find innovative new techniques and workflows, as well as reworked solutions that take advantage of new developments.

Brian P. Hogan, Chris Warren, Mike Weber, and Chris Johnson
(358 pages) ISBN: 9781680500561. $38
https://pragprog.com/book/wbdev2

Practical Vim, Second Edition

Vim is a fast and efficient text editor that will make you a faster and more efficient developer. It's available on almost every OS, and if you master the techniques in this book, you'll never need another text editor. In more than 120 Vim tips, you'll quickly learn the editor's core functionality and tackle your trickiest editing and writing tasks. This beloved bestseller has been revised and updated to Vim 8 and includes three brand-new tips and five fully revised tips.

Drew Neil
(354 pages) ISBN: 9781680501278. $29
https://pragprog.com/book/dnvim2

Pragmatic Programming

We'll show you how to be more pragmatic and effective, for new code and old.

Your Code as a Crime Scene

Jack the Ripper and legacy codebases have more in common than you'd think. Inspired by forensic psychology methods, this book teaches you strategies to predict the future of your codebase, assess refactoring direction, and understand how your team influences the design. With its unique blend of forensic psychology and code analysis, this book arms you with the strategies you need, no matter what programming language you use.

Adam Tornhill
(218 pages) ISBN: 9781680500387. $36
https://pragprog.com/book/atcrime

The Nature of Software Development

You need to get value from your software project. You need it "free, now, and perfect." We can't get you there, but we can help you get to "cheaper, sooner, and better." This book leads you from the desire for value down to the specific activities that help good Agile projects deliver better software sooner, and at a lower cost. Using simple sketches and a few words, the author invites you to follow his path of learning and understanding from a half century of software development and from his engagement with Agile methods from their very beginning.

Ron Jeffries
(176 pages) ISBN: 9781941222379. $24
https://pragprog.com/book/rjnsd

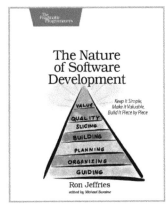

Secure and Better JavaScript

Secure your Node applications and make writing JavaScript easier and more productive.

Secure Your Node.js Web Application

Cyber-criminals have your web applications in their crosshairs. They search for and exploit common security mistakes in your web application to steal user data. Learn how you can secure your Node.js applications, database and web server to avoid these security holes. Discover the primary attack vectors against web applications, and implement security best practices and effective countermeasures. Coding securely will make you a stronger web developer and analyst, and you'll protect your users.

Karl Düüna
(230 pages) ISBN: 9781680500851. $36
https://pragprog.com/book/kdnodesec

CoffeeScript

Over the last five years, CoffeeScript has taken the web development world by storm. With the humble motto "It's just JavaScript," CoffeeScript provides all the power of the JavaScript language in a friendly and elegant package. This extensively revised and updated new edition includes an all-new project to demonstrate CoffeeScript in action, both in the browser and on a Node.js server. There's no faster way to learn to write a modern web application.

Trevor Burnham
(122 pages) ISBN: 9781941222263. $29
https://pragprog.com/book/tbcoffee2

Start Great Teams, Keep Teams Great

See how to get great teams started, and keep them great by doing retrospectives the right way.

Liftoff, Second Edition

Ready, set, liftoff! Align your team to one purpose: successful delivery. Learn new insights and techniques for starting projects and teams the right way, with expanded concepts for planning, organizing, and conducting liftoff meetings. Real-life stories illustrate how others have effectively started (or restarted) their teams and projects. Master coaches Diana Larsen and Ainsley Nies have successfully "lifted off" numerous agile projects worldwide. Are you ready for success?

Diana Larsen and Ainsley Nies
(170 pages) ISBN: 9781680501636. $24
https://pragprog.com/book/liftoff

Agile Retrospectives

See how to mine the experience of your software development team continually throughout the life of the project. The tools and recipes in this book will help you uncover and solve hidden (and not-so-hidden) problems with your technology, your methodology, and those difficult "people issues" on your team.

Esther Derby and Diana Larsen, Foreword by Ken Schwaber
(176 pages) ISBN: 9780977616640. $29.95
https://pragprog.com/book/dlret

Past and Present

To see where we're going, remember how we got here, and learn how to take a healthier approach to programming.

Fire in the Valley

In the 1970s, while their contemporaries were protesting the computer as a tool of dehumanization and oppression, a motley collection of college dropouts, hippies, and electronics fanatics were engaged in something much more subversive. Obsessed with the idea of getting computer power into their own hands, they launched from their garages a hobbyist movement that grew into an industry, and ultimately a social and technological revolution. What they did was invent the personal computer: not just a new device, but a watershed in the relationship between man and machine. This is their story.

Michael Swaine and Paul Freiberger
(422 pages) ISBN: 9781937785765. $34
https://pragprog.com/book/fsfire

The Healthy Programmer

To keep doing what you love, you need to maintain your own systems, not just the ones you write code for. Regular exercise and proper nutrition help you learn, remember, concentrate, and be creative—skills critical to doing your job well. Learn how to change your work habits, master exercises that make working at a computer more comfortable, and develop a plan to keep fit, healthy, and sharp for years to come.

This book is intended only as an informative guide for those wishing to know more about health issues. In no way is this book intended to replace, countermand, or conflict with the advice given to you by your own healthcare provider including Physician, Nurse Practitioner, Physician Assistant, Registered Dietician, and other licensed professionals.

Joe Kutner
(254 pages) ISBN: 9781937785314. $36
https://pragprog.com/book/jkthp

The Pragmatic Bookshelf

The Pragmatic Bookshelf features books written by developers for developers. The titles continue the well-known Pragmatic Programmer style and continue to garner awards and rave reviews. As development gets more and more difficult, the Pragmatic Programmers will be there with more titles and products to help you stay on top of your game.

Visit Us Online

This Book's Home Page
https://pragprog.com/book/bhtmux2
Source code from this book, errata, and other resources. Come give us feedback, too!

Keep Up to Date
https://pragprog.com
Join our announcement mailing list (low volume) or follow us on twitter @pragprog for new titles, sales, coupons, hot tips, and more.

New and Noteworthy
https://pragprog.com/news
Check out the latest pragmatic developments, new titles and other offerings.

Contact Us

Online Orders:	*https://pragprog.com/catalog*
Customer Service:	*support@pragprog.com*
International Rights:	*translations@pragprog.com*
Academic Use:	*academic@pragprog.com*
Write for Us:	*http://write-for-us.pragprog.com*
Or Call:	+1 800-699-7764

9 781680 502213